William S. Kervin is Assista ... Emmanuel College in Toront ... of The United Church of Cana ... ... and overseas ministries and be ... ... the development of the worship resources of his denomination. He is the author of *The Language of Baptism* (Scarecrow Press, 2003) and numerous articles on liturgy and worship, and is a frequent preacher, presider, lecturer and workshop leader.

A Year of Grace

365 Mealtime Prayers

William S. Kervin

Foreword by John L. Bell

First published in Great Britain in 2003 by
Society for Promoting Christian Knowledge
Holy Trinity Church
Marylebone Road
London NW1 4DU

Acknowledgements for the use of copyright material reproduced in
this book are on pp. 128–40.

British Library Cataloguing-in-Publication Data
A catalogue record for this book is available
from the British Library

ISBN 0-281-05628-5

1 3 5 7 9 10 8 6 4 2

Typeset by Avocet Typeset, Chilton, Aylesbury, Bucks
Printed in Great Britain by Richard Clay Ltd., St Ives plc

for
Linda Grace Huestis

Contents

Foreword

One of the great mysteries of faith to which my thoughts recurrently turn is why we make Jesus out to be so skinny.

From a thousand stained-glass windows, from an equal number of renaissance and contemporary paintings, and from our own conditioned imaginations we turn the Saviour of the World into a humourless rake. And all this as if he were not the son of a Jewish mother who liked parties and who launched him into his public ministry when the wine ran out at a wedding feast.

If there is no smoke without fire, then the mere fact that Jesus was called a 'glutton and a drunkard' must surely alert us to the gregarious nature which was in Christ and which should be in his followers. Maybe it is the solemnity which surrounds the Last Supper and the incredulity which accompanies the Feeding of the Five Thousand which distract us from the dozen other venues where Jesus blessed food and shared it. Or maybe parsimonious religion has convinced us that it is both preferable and cheaper to fast than to feast.

Whatever the reason, the depiction of Christ as emaciated and the individualism of our age require people of faith to rediscover the centrality of the table, of feeding and eating and sharing hospitality.

And what better place to start than with a book of graces, which in their diversity of origin, subject matter and style allow us not only to bless our food, but also to savour the history, geography, variety and integrity of Christian gratitude.

There is no better commendation for this book than that the author has gathered together what he has prayed, and that in producing this volume he responded to a need which he and many others have felt. God is worth more and our food is worth more than two grudged phrases muttered apologetically. So I warmly welcome and endorse this lovely book of graces. May they be as good for our souls as the food they bless is good for our bodies.

John L. Bell

Preface

This is a simple book with a simple goal in mind: to pray one brief prayer, each day, at mealtimes.

For years now I have kept on the lookout for such a book. Along the way, many fine collections have inspired my own prayers at table. But, in the end, my simple goal became also, I suppose, a rather personal and biased one. I longed for an uncluttered volume, physically and spiritually – a prayer a day for 365 days; prayers that would be not too earnest, but often humorous; not too sentimental, but often political. I imagined an attractive little volume that would have a home on the table in a kitchen or dining room. It could be passed from hand to hand as loved ones, friends, strangers and guests gathered to break bread together. It could be opened when alone at mealtime and perhaps play a part in making the difference between loneliness and solitude. It could also be given as a gift, thus embodying something of the grace of which it attempts to speak. I imagined giving it to my family, friends and colleagues, who grace my life. How close this volume comes to these ideals remains to be seen, but I am pleased to be able to offer it, such as it is.

The criterion for the selection of these prayers has been equally simple, biased, even selfish: I like them! They are all prayers that I can pray. This means that most of them (but not all) use inclusive language with respect to God and persons. Some of them (but not enough) struggle to pray about the inequities of life and the problem of hunger in the global village. Others (nowhere near enough) seek to bring before God a desire to live in right relationship with creation.

Many of them draw on hymn texts, where some of the best language of prayer is often found. Others come from historical and literary sources. Some have been chosen in the hope that children can use them. A few are, strictly speaking, not even prayers – which is to say, they do not address God directly. In this I have interpreted prayer liberally: words which draw us into an awareness of the presence of the Divine.

Most of the prayers are Christian. While this reflects my location in the life of faith, I have not felt it necessary to stop there. Thus, some pluralistic influence is evident, even if this was not the primary goal of the collection. Books of interfaith prayers of all kinds are available and to be commended to all who pray. In this particular collection an excerpt from one of the Psalms is used for every seventh prayer, thus acknowledging something of the sabbath rhythm shared by many faiths. I, for one, pray the Psalms thankful that they are texts shared by Jews, Christians and Muslims. The particular translation of the Psalms used is based on the version found in *Voices United: The Hymn and Worship Book of The United Church of Canada*, with some adaptations using the New Revised Standard Version (NRSV) of the Bible. Otherwise, the prayers are arranged somewhat randomly.

To be sure, there are more sophisticated ways to organize such a book and more credible criteria for selection. The liturgical scholar in me is somewhat embarrassed by the simple (simplistic?) approach of this volume. It bears no relationship, for example, to the Revised Common Lectionary or the seasons of the liturgical calendar. Nevertheless, I find myself attracted to its utility: a prayer a day. Begin on any day. The important thing is that we just begin.

It is my hope that others will continue to extemporize and improvise on this material – prayer being, after all, a living language of life, not limited to printed texts but often supported and disciplined by forms of prayer.

I want to acknowledge my debt to the sources cited at the back of this volume. I have borrowed and adapted liberally, and while the permissions of many have been generously granted, it is I who must bear responsibility for the final results.

In addition, I want to thank my colleagues and students at Emmanuel College, Toronto, who continue to inspire and challenge me daily in the work of faith and the living out of grace. I suspect that Marilyn Legge, Phyllis Airhart, Michael Bourgeois, Karen Wishart and Lynda Katsuno have no idea about the extent to which their suggestions and passing comments sparked the inspiration and energy required to see this project through. John Ambrose, Fred Graham, Abigail Johnson and Peter Wyatt have been particularly encouraging. Thorough research assistance was given by Lori Cotnam and financial support came from Emmanuel College and the Senate of Victoria University.

A special word of thanks and appreciation is due to John Bell, friend, colleague and inspiration. Having his Foreword grace this volume of 'wee prayers' (as he would call them) is a great gift. John and the Iona Community continue to be a prophetic witness to the integration of worship and work, prayer and politics. As the pages of this volume show, I am deeply indebted to his and their work.

Last, yet first, from the beginning I imagined this little book as primarily a gift to Linda, with whom I break bread daily and whose middle name, Grace, describes my life with her, 365 days a year. This is for her.

365 Prayers

O God, our God,

    how glorious is your name in all the earth!

From the lips of infants and children

    your praises reach up to the heavens.

When I look to the heavens,

    the work of your fingers,

    the moon and the stars you have set

      in their places,

what are we mortals

    that you should be mindful of us,

mere human beings

    that you should care for us?

O God, our God,

    how glorious is your name in all the earth!

from Psalm 8

God of grace and passion,

for companions,

    make us joyful;

2

for food,

    make us thankful;

and for justice

    make us hungry.

Amen.

WSK

3   Blest are those who from this table
        live their days in gratitude.
    Taste and see the grace eternal.
        Taste and see that God is good.

Sylvia G. Dunstan

4   We are thankful for these
        and all the good things of life.
    We recognize that they are part of our common heritage,
        and come to us through the efforts
        of our brothers and sisters the world over.
    To this end, may we take our share in the world's work
        and the world's struggle.
    Amen.

attrib. J. S. Woodsworth

5   God of grace,
        let love be the sweetness
    and wisdom the seasoning
        at this table.
    Amen.

Sister Mary Teresa, OP

6   Now thank we all our God,
        with heart, and hands, and voices,
    who wondrous things has done,

in whom this world rejoices;
who from our mother's arms
   has blessed us on our way
with countless gifts of love,
   and still is ours today.
Amen.

Martin Rinckart, 1636

O our Father, the Sky, hear us,   7
   and open us to your mystery.
O our Mother, the Earth, hear us,
   and feed us with your goodness.
O Spirit of the East, hear us,
   send us your Wisdom.
O Spirit of the South, hear us,
   guide us on the path of life.
O Spirit of the West, hear us,
   make us always ready for the long journey.
O Spirit of the North, hear us,
   purify us with your cleansing winds.
Father, Mother, Spirit, hear us,
   as we talk of your ways
   and take of your food.
Amen.

Sioux Grace, alt.

I will give thanks to you, God,   8
   with my whole heart;
I will tell of all your marvellous deeds.

I will be glad and rejoice in you;
I will sing praise to your name,
O Most High.

from Psalm 9

9   God of life and peace,
        may this food
        nourish body and soul,
        honouring its Source
        and seeking its goal:
            flesh fed,
            spirits sustained,
            a world renewed.
Amen.

WSK

10   God is my shepherd,
        I'll not want,
        I feed in pastures green.
God grants me rest
        and bids me drink
        from waters calm and clean.
Through daily tasks,
        I'm blessed and led
        by one I have not seen.
Amen.

*Scottish Psalter, 1650,
adapt. Lavon Bayler*

With bread
   and wine,
we can walk the road.
Thanks be to God.

Spanish Proverb

11

Bless, O God,
   this food and drink,
   all drawn from your creation.
May it nourish us
   for your work
   of peace and liberation.
Amen.

Betty Lynn Schwab

12

May the yams which our sisters and brothers
   plant in the earth this year be good.
May children be born.
May all have enough to eat,
   and may peace reign.
Amen.

Nigerian, alt.

13

God, receive our thanks
   for the gifts of many seasons,
   and the service of many hands.
Amen.

Rita F. Snowden

14

15   My trust is in your mercy, O God.
My heart rejoices in your salvation.
I will sing to you, O God,
    because you have dealt bountifully with me.
I will praise your name,
    O God most high.

from Psalm 13

16   Let us break bread,
    praying that the kingdom of God
    may break into our world.
Let us pour wine,
    praying that God's justice
    will roll down
    like an ever-flowing stream.
And let us open our hearts
    to behold this promise,
    and open our hands
    to share it.
Amen.

WSK

17   Praise God for Brother Sun,
    light, lovely, glowing and guiding.
Praise God for Sister Wind,
    clear or cloudy, caressing and moving.
Praise God for Brother Fire,
    warm comfort, burning and warming.

Praise God for Sister Water,
  precious and deep, bathing and renewing.
Praise God for Mother Earth,
  raising food to feed us
  and giving us life.
Amen.

St Francis of Assisi

For beauty of prairies,   18
  for grandeur of trees,
for flowers of woodlands,
  for creatures of seas,
for all you created
  and gave us to share,
we praise you, Creator,
  extolling your care.
Amen.

Walter Farquharson

Embracing God,   19
  your gospel claims one family
    with a billion names;
  let every life be touched by grace
    until we praise you face to face.
Amen.

Jeffrey W. Rowthorn
© 1978 Hope Publishing/Copycare
music@copycare.com

20   Bless the calloused hands of migrant workers.
       Bless the flour-covered fingers of bakers.
       Bless the feel and aroma of food.
       Bless those who gather.
       Bless the breaking of bread.
       Blessed Be!

       William John Fitzgerald, alt.

21   Bread is broken —
            friendship's token.
       In our sharing
            love is shown.
       Wine is given —
            laughter, leaven.
       At this table
            God is known.
       Amen.

       *Diane Taylor and
       Ken Powers, alt.*

22   You, O God,
            show me the path of life.
       In your presence
            there is fullness of joy;
       and from your hand
            flow pleasures for evermore.

       from Psalm 16

The hands around this table   23
    remind us of
hands that weed the fields
    and tend the livestock
    and haul the nets;
hands that pack the boxes
    and load the trucks
    and stock the shelves;
hands that work where we do not,
    like the very hands of God.
For this and so much more,
    we are deeply thankful.
Amen.
WSK

For the fruit of all creation,   24
    thanks be to God.
For the gifts to every nation,
    thanks be to God.
For the ploughing, sowing, reaping,
    silent growth while we are sleeping,
future needs in earth's safe-keeping,
    thanks be to God.

In the just reward of labour,
    God's will is done.
In the help we give our neighbour,
    God's will is done.
In our world-wide task of caring
    for the hungry and despairing,

in the harvests we are sharing,
    God's will is done.

For the harvests of the Spirit,
    thanks be to God.
For the good we all inherit,
    thanks be to God.
For the wonders that astound us,
    for the truths that still confound us,
most of all that love has found us,
    thanks be to God.

Fred Pratt Green

25   Give us, O God, of the morning meal,
    benefit to the body, the frame of the soul;
Give us, O God, of the broken bread,
    enough for our need at the evening close.
Amen.

Celtic

26   Holy God, Holy One, Holy Three!
You beyond the galaxies,
You under the oceans,
You inside the leaves,
You pouring down rain,
You opening the flowers,
You feeding the insects,
You giving us your image,
You carrying us through the waters,

You holding us in the night,
Your smile on Sarah and Abraham,
Your hand with Moses and Miriam,
Your words through Deborah and Isaiah,
You lived as Jesus among us,
Healing, teaching, dying, rising,
Inviting us all to your feast.
Amen.

Gail Ramshaw

To God who gives our daily bread   27
    a thankful song we raise,
and pray the One who sends us food
    may fill our hearts with praise.
Amen.

Thomas Tallis, 16th century, alt.

God, bless our shared meal,   28
    a sacrament of our debt
    to all creation.
Amen.

Mount St Mary's Abbey, alt.

It was you who took me   29
    from the womb;
you kept me safe
    on my mother's breast.

On you
   I was cast from my birth;
since my mother bore me,
   you have been my God.

from Psalm 22

30   Come, Spirit of Wisdom,
        and be our guest,
     our table be graced,
     our food be blessed.
     Amen.

     WSK

31   Mothering Spirit,
        nurturing one,
           in arms of patience hold us close,
     so that in faith we root and grow
        until we flower, until we know.
     Praise and thanks be to you, our Mother.
     Amen.

     Julian of Norwich, 14th century,
     adapt. Jean Wiebe Janzen

32   God, we thank you
        that we are able to eat together.
     Be also with those who eat alone.
     Amen.

     German

God is gracious,   33
God is good,
   let us give thanks
   for our food.
Through these hands
may all be fed;
   make us, God,
   your daily bread.
Amen.

Jan L. Richardson

O Lord, that lends me life,   34
   lend me a heart replete with thankfulness.
Amen.

William Shakespeare

Blessed art Thou, O Lord our God,   35
King of the universe,
   who creates many living beings
   and the things they need.
For all that Thou hast created
   to sustain the life of every living being,
   blessed be Thou,
   the Life of the universe.
Amen.

Jewish

36   You, God, spread a table for me
          in the sight of my enemies;
      you anoint my head with oil;
          my cup is overflowing.
      from Psalm 23

37   Ever-present God,
          you come to us in the stranger's guise
          and are known in every breaking of bread.
      Open us to your presence
          in the faces of all whom we meet,
      that we may see
          in every welcome extended
          and in all food shared
          communion with you.
      It is for the sake of your whole human family,
          that we pray that this may be so.
      Amen.
      WSK

38   May God, as Shepherd of the sheep,
          protect and bless us while we eat.
      And, as God's sheep, we safely graze,
          for bounty give thanks, all our days.
      Amen.
      Woolmen's Company Grace, alt.

Thou spread'st a table in my sight;   39
    thy unction grace bestoweth;
and O what transport of delight
    from thy pure chalice floweth!
Amen.

Henry Williams Baker, 1869

Creator, Earth Mother,   40
Guardians and Keepers of the four directions,
    we thank you for this day in our lives,
    we thank you for the lives of all that gave away
        that we may live —
    the animal and plant people.
May we live our lives in a way that
    they would be proud of our continuing energy.
All my relations.

Wind Daughter, Medicine Chief of the
Bear Tribe Medicine Society

Give us this day our daily bread, O God,   41
    and grant that we who are filled
        with good things
    from your open hand
may never close our hearts to
    the hungry,
    the homeless,
    and the poor.
Amen.

Abbey of New Clairvaux

42   O God, who makes a thousand flowers to blow,
who makes both grains and fruits to grow,
hear our prayer:
>bless this food
>>and bring us peace.

Amen.

Dutch

43   The earth is God's,
>and all that is in it;

the world,
>and those who live upon it.

from Psalm 24

44   God of celebration and lamentation,
>our every gathering at table
>reminds us of the blessings and burdens
>>of this world,
>the gift and grief of this life.

And so we pause before we eat
>to remember those who do not eat.

Keep us always
>thankful
>and mindful.

Amen.

WSK

Father, we thank Thee for the night,   45
    and for the pleasant morning light.
For rest and food and loving care,
    and all that makes the day so fair.

Help us to do the things we should,
    to be to others kind and good;
in all we do, in all we say,
    to grow more loving every day.
Amen.
Rebecca J. Weston

Joy to those who come.   46
Peace to those who eat.
Blessings to those who leave.
Methodist chapel, Hawkshead,
England, alt.

Holy God, Holy One, Holy Three,   47
Our Life, our Mercy, our Might,
Our Table, our Food, our Server,
Our Rainbow, our Ark, our Dove,
Our Sovereign, our Water, our Wine,
Our Light, our Treasure, our Tree,
Our Way, our Truth, our Life.
Praise now,
Praise tomorrow,
Praise forever.
Amen.
Gail Ramshaw

48   Bless these thy gifts, most gracious God,
        from whom all goodness springs;
make clean our hearts and feed our souls
        with good and joyful things.
Amen.

Elizabethan Primer, 1580

49   Then God, gathering up her courage in love, said,
'Let there be bread!'
And God's sisters,
        her friends and lovers
        knelt on the earth
        planted the seeds
        prayed for the rain
        sang for the grain
        made the harvest
        cracked the wheat
        pounded the corn
        kneaded the dough
        kindled the fire
        filled the air
        with the smell of fresh bread
And there was bread!
And it was good!

We the sisters of God say today,
        'All shall eat of the bread,
        And the power.'
We say today,
        'All shall have power
        And bread.'

Today we say,
'Let there be bread!
Let there be power!
Let us eat of the bread
    and the power!
And all will be filled
For the bread is rising!'
Carter Heyward

Blessed be God,   50
    Most High,
who has wondrously shown
    steadfast love to me.
from Psalm 31

Here are two simple words to inspire our   51
    prayers at table:
    companion — which means, literally, one
        who shares bread;
    humility — which means, literally, of the earth.
And so we pray:
Sacred Spirit,
    make us companions,
    and keep us humble,
        with others
        and for the earth.
Amen.
WSK

19

52   Mothering God,
          you gave us birth
          in the bright morning of this world.
      Creator, source of every breath,
          you are our rain,
          our wind,
          our sun.
      Praise and thanks be to you, our Mother.
      Amen.

      Julian of Norwich, 14th century,
      adapt. Jean Wiebe Janzen

53   God, we praise you for creation,
          mountains, seas, and prairie land.
      Waking souls find joy and healing
          in your bountiful hand.
      Amen.

      Jim Strathdee

54   Blessed are you, O God,
          who brings forth the bread of hospitality
          from the earth.
      You made us to be
          companions,
          sharers of bread,
      to gather
          and to break
          and to be astonished
          by the flavour breaking forth.

Bless to us
   this meal
   that by its sharing
we too may gasp
   at your Spirit's breaking forth
   in us.
Amen.

Jan L. Richardson

Earth, water, air, and fire   55
   combined to make this food.
Numberless beings have died and laboured
   that we may eat.
May we be nourished
   that we may nourish life.
Amen.

Ojai School

Some have food.   56
Some have none.
God bless the revolution!
Amen.

Beverly Wildung Harrison

O magnify God with me,   57
   let us exalt God's name together.
Taste and see
   that our God is good.

from Psalm 34

58   For food and feasting,
    we thank you
      and pray.
    For laughter and love,
    we praise you
      and pray.
    For freedom and peace,
    we bless you
      and pray.
    Amen.
    WSK

59   Be thankful for the least gift,
      so shalt thou be meet to receive the greater.
    Thanks be to God.
    Thomas à Kempis, 15th century

60   Taste and see
      the grace eternal.
    Taste and see
      that God is good!
    Amen.
    Sylvia G. Dunstan

Thank Heaven for this food 61
    and for this company.
May it be good for us.
Amen.
Greek

These mercies bless, 62
    and grant that we
may feast in Paradise
    with thee.
Amen.
Howard Spring

For this food 63
    and joy renewed,
we praise your name,
    O God.
Amen.
A Monk's Table Prayer, alt.

How precious 64
    is your steadfast love, O God!
All people may take refuge
    in the shadow of your wings.

They feast
　　on the abundance of your house,
and you give them drink
　　from the river of your delights.

from Psalm 36

65　　We thank you, God,
　　　　that such simple things
　　　　as food and friendship
　　　　can accomplish such profound work.
　　Through these gifts
　　　　you nourish our bodies,
　　　　and nurture our very souls;
　　you bring happiness to this home,
　　　　and hope and healing to the world.
　　Thanks be to you, O God,
　　　　for food and friendship.
　　Amen.

WSK

66　　Come, Lord Jesus, be our guest,
　　　　and may our meal by you be blest.
　　Amen.

Martin Luther, 16th century

67　　The food which we are about to eat
　　　　is Earth, Water, and Sun,
　　　　compounded through the alchemy of many plants.
　　Therefore Earth, Water and Sun
　　　　will become part of us.

This food is also
    the fruit of the labour of many beings
    and creatures.
We are grateful for it.
May it give us strength, health, joy.
And may it increase our love.
Amen.
Unitarian

We are thankful for this meal,   68
    the work of many people
    and the sharing of other forms of life.
Zen, alt.

If we have earned the right to eat this bread,   69
    happy indeed are we;
but if unmerited thou givest to us,
    may we more thankful be.
Amen.
Girl Guide Grace

Eternal Spirit of Justice and Love,   70
    as we come to this table,
    make us aware of our dependence on the earth
    and on the sustaining presence
    of other human beings,
    both living and gone before us.

As we partake of this food and drink,
    help us remember that there are many for whom
    sufficient bread is a luxury,
    or for whom wine, when attainable,
    is only an escape.
Transform our thanksgiving for life's bounty
    into commitment to changing the world,
    that those who are now hungry may be filled
    and those without hope may be given courage.
Amen.
Congregation of Abraxas, alt.

71   With you, O God,
            is the fountain of life;
        in your light
            do we see light.
        Continue your steadfast love,
            O God.
        from Psalm 36

72   Blessed are you,
            great and gracious God,
            Creator of light,
            Giver of all life,
            Source of love.
        You guide the sun,
            and cradle the moon,
            and toss the stars —
            yet sit among us here.

Blessed are you,
  great and gracious God,
  who blesses us.
Amen.
WSK and Lillian Perigoe

Good Lord for thy Grace meekly we call,   73
  bless us and our meals and drinks withal.
Amen.
Salisbury Primer, 1536

Let us praise the God of truth,   74
  let us praise the God of peace,
    let us praise the God of love.
Amen.
Mungakan (Cameroon)

Blessed be God for our kinship —   75
  with all races and creeds,
  and with all God's creatures.
God looks upon us all,
  as we look upon this table,
  and it is all very good!
Amen.
William John Fitzgerald

76   For food and friends
        and all you send,
    we praise your holy name.
    Amen.

Anonymous

77   Blessed be thou, Lord God of the universe,
        who bringest forth bread from the earth,
        and makest glad the hearts of your people.
    Amen.

Traditional Jewish

78   O God, my God,
        you have multiplied your wondrous deeds
        and your thoughts towards us.
    None can compare with you!
    I would proclaim and tell of them,
        but they are more
        than can be numbered.

from Psalm 40

79   Creator God,
    Artisan of all that is,
        we thank you
            for the soil under foot
                and the stars over head;
            for the fruits of earth and sky,
                field and sea.

Your every work
    blesses body and soul,
        heart and mind.
And so we bless you;
    and we pray that you would fashion in us
        two things more:
            humility
            and generosity.
Even in the face of all your gifts to us,
    may this too be so.
Amen.
WSK

Be the meal of beans or peas,   80
    God be thanked for those and these.
Have we flesh or have we fish,
    all are fragments from God's dish.
And our peace here, like a spring,
    make it ever flourishing.
Amen.
Elizabethan Children's Grace, 16th century

Blessed be God, King of the Universe,   81
    who has created all things living,
    and has supplied the means
    to sustain the life of each of them.
Blessed be God,
the life of all the world.
Amen.
Jewish

82 Gather us in,
  at this and every table,
   to meet, to eat,
   be given a seat,
   be joined to the vine,
   be offered new wine,
   become like the least,
   be found at the feast.
 Amen.

John L. Bell,
Iona Community, alt.

83 For every cup and plate full,
  God make us truly grateful.
 Amen.

Anonymous

84 Gracious God,
  you have created the countryside:
  its fields and forests,
  hills and rivers,
  birds and animals
  and fresh, healthy air to breathe.
 We thank you for all this goodness and beauty.

 Help those for whom rural life is hard and difficult:
  those who must travel far to collect firewood
  and bring their water from distant streams;
  all who live in poor conditions.

Bless the efforts being made to improve
    conditions in rural areas,
  so that the people who work
    to feed the nations
  may themselves enjoy a higher standard
    of living.
Amen.
Kenyan

Like a deer that longs for life-giving waters,   85
  so longs my soul for you, O God.
My soul thirsts for you, O God.
My soul thirsts for you,
  the source of my life.
from Psalm 42

Bless to us, O God,   86
  the bread of satisfaction,
  and the cup of longing.
Feed our hunger today,
  but keep us thirsty
  for a new tomorrow.
Amen.
WSK

87   Great God, thou Giver of all good,
       accept our praise and bless our food:
grace, health and strength to us afford
       through Jesus Christ, our risen Lord.
Amen.

Jeremiah Clarke, 17th century

88   Jesus, our Friend,
       it's good to know
       that you lived in the flesh,
       walked where we walk,
       felt what we feel,
       had sore and dirty feet,
       and needed to eat.
But it's even better to know
       that you enjoyed your food,
       the feel of perfume on your skin,
       the wind on your face,
       a child in your arms,
       and good wine at the wedding.
Thank you for sharing in all our pain and pleasure;
       and thank you for joining us at this table.
Amen.

Kathy Galloway, Iona Community, alt.

89   And forgive us, Lord,
       for not knowing how to share the bread
       which you have given us,
as we forgive those
who have taken from us your bread
which is ours.

Forgive us for separating ourselves
   from our brothers.
Forgive us, Lord, for our lack
   of faith and courage
   which prevents us from surrendering ourselves as
      living hosts
   to do your will,
which is to take what is yours
   and share it with everyone right now.
Forgive us when out of fear
   we remain silent
   and do not say what you want us to say.
Forgive and destroy
   the tiny kingdoms
   and the useless struggles
   which exist among us,
   which delay and obstruct our victorious march
   towards the New Dawn.
Amen.

Julia Esquivel (Lord's Prayer from Guatemala)

Receive our thanks   90
   for night and day,
for food and shelter,
   rest and play.
Be here our guest
   and with us stay.
Amen.

Refuge Blessing

91   For health,
            for food,
            and for the work of others,
       we thank you, God.
       Amen.

Anonymous

92   I am like a thriving olive tree
            in God's house;
       I will praise you forever,
            for all you have done.

from Psalm 52

93   Bless to us, O God,
            the doors we open,
            the guests we welcome,
            the tables we set,
            the food we share,
            and the roads which lie ahead.
       Amen.

WSK, based on Kate McIlhagga,
Iona Community

94   Back of the bread is the flour.
            Back of the flour is the mill.
       And back of the mill is the wind and the rain
            and God's gracious will.
       Amen.

Miller's Grace

Thanks be to God, who doth now send   95
    the ample board, the honest friend —
the social joys of wit and mirth,
    all good companionship on earth.
Amen.

Anonymous

'Wisdom has built her house;   96
she has hewn seven pillars,
she has prepared the meal;
she has set her table and sent out her servants.
She calls from the highest places in the town:
"Come, eat of my bread,
and drink of the wine I have mixed." '
Sophia be praised!
Thanks be to you, Holy Wisdom!
Amen.

Wisdom Grace, based on Proverbs 8

Here is bread,   97
    which strengthens the heart,
and is therefore called
    the staff of life.
Thanks be to God.

Matthew Henry, 17th century

You, O God,   98
    are mighty and gracious forever.
You cause the wind to blow
    and the rain to fall.

You sustain the living,
   give life to the dead,
   support the falling,
   free those who are bound,
   and keep your faith with the lowly.
Who is like unto you,
   O God of mighty acts?
Praise be to you forever.
Amen.

Traditional Jewish, alt.

99   See, God is my helper;
it is God
   who upholds my life.

from Psalm 54

100   May the Maker's blessing be upon us at this table,
   gathering us in,
   drawing us close,
   embracing us,
   enfolding us.
May the Son's blessing be upon us at this table,
   in wine and water,
   in bread and stories,
   to feed us,
   to remind us.

May the Spirit's blessing be upon us at this table,
    the movement,
    the warmth,
    the nurture,
    the vision.
And may our own blessings be upon one another,
    blessings rooted in our common pilgrimage,
    the benediction of friends,
    hand in hand.
Amen.

WSK, based on Ruth Burgess,
Iona Community

May God's bounty feed us   101
and God's Light guide us
    till our sailing ends.
Amen.

Sailors' Grace

Thank you, God,   102
    for this fine day.
Bless our food,
    our work,
    our play.
Amen.

Anonymous

103   Blessing of heaven — cloud blessing,
blessing of earth — fruit blessing,
blessing of sea — fish blessing,
blessing of sun — light blessing,
blessing of moon — night blessing,
blessing of ale — food blessing,
blessing of light — dew blessing,
blessing of wisdom — valour blessing,
blessing of grain — plough blessing.
Amen.

Cashel Blessing

104   For brimming plate
    and flowing cup
and hands that help
    in washing up,
we give you thanks,
    O God.
Amen.

Anonymous

105   We thank you, God,
    for happy hearts,
    for rain and sunny weather.
We thank you for the food we eat,
    and for the time together.
Amen.

Anonymous

Awake, my soul!   106
    Awake, O harp and lyre!
I will awake the dawn.
I will give thanks to you, O God,
    among the peoples;
I will sing praises to you
    among the nations.
For your steadfast love
    is as high as the heavens;
your faithfulness
    extends to the clouds.
from Psalm 57

Thank you for the food we share,   107
    the sun and rain that helped it grow.
Thank you, God, for all your gifts,
    all the kindness that you show.
Amen.
WSK

For health and food,   108
    for love and friends;
for everything
    Thy goodness sends,
we thank Thee.
Amen.
Ralph Waldo Emerson,
19th century

109 God of grace,
   may our food receive blessing,
   may our table show welcome,
   may our talk know compassion,
   may our prayers be for peace.
  Amen.
  WSK

110 O gracious God,
   when you open your hand,
   you satisfy the desires
   of every living thing.
  Bless the land and waters;
   give the world a plentiful harvest;
   let your spirit go forth
   to renew the face of the earth.
  As you show your love and kindness
   in the bounty of the land and sea,
   save us from selfish use of your gifts,
   so that women and men everywhere
   may live in harmony.
  Amen.
  Holden Village

111 God bless our going out,
   nor less our coming in,
   and make them sure.

God bless our daily bread,
    and bless whate'er we do,
    whate'er endure.
Amen.

Prince Albert, 19th century, alt.

God, our Creator, 112
    you prepare for us this table,
    and our cup overflows with blessing.
God, our Way,
    you give us bread for the journey
    and the sweet wine of arrival.
God, our Companion,
    you give us manna in the wilderness,
    and quench our thirst in the desert.
For your blessing,
    your care
    and your promise,
    we give you thanks.
Amen.

WSK and Janet Cawley

O my strength, 113
    I will sing praises to you,
for you, O God,
    are my fortress,
the God who shows me
    steadfast love.

from Psalm 59

114   Holy God, Holy One, Holy Three,
        all things come together here:
            food and faith,
            body and soul,
            flesh and spirit.
    Bless this food.
    Bless its journey to this table.
    And bless our efforts to do it justice.
    Amen.
    WSK

115   This day God gives me
        strength of high heaven,
        sun and moon shining,
        flame in the hearth,
        flashing of lightning,
        wind in its swiftness,
        deeps of the ocean,
        firmness of earth.
    Amen.
    attrib. St Patrick

116   With this food, O God,
        comes your blessing and keeping:
        from morning's waking
        till night's folding,
        comings and goings,
        the spinning of labour and life.

God bless this food,
  this day,
  this work,
  this journey.
May we and those we meet
  be better for it.
Amen.

WSK,
based on William John Fitzgerald

Bless us, O Lord, and these thy gifts   117
  which through thy bounty we are about
  to receive through Christ our Lord.
Amen.

Traditional, anonymous

God of the sparrow   118
God of the whale
God of the swirling stars
How does the creature say Awe
How does the creature say Praise

God of the hungry
God of the sick
God of the prodigal
How does the creature say Care
How does the creature say Life

God of the rainbow
God of the cross
God of the empty grave
How does the creature say Grace
How does the creature say Thanks.
Amen.

Jaroslav J. Vajda
© 1984 CPH. Used with permission

119   *Everyone at the table joins hands for a silent*
           moment, ending with:
       Amen.

Quaker

120   I will give thanks
            as long as I live;
       I will lift up my hands
            and call on your name.
       My soul is satisfied
            as with a rich feast,
       and my mouth praises you
            with joyful lips.

from Psalm 63

121   Sophia, we pray:
            prepare the feast
            and set the table
       with justice for bread
            and peace for wine.
       Amen.

WSK, based on Jan L. Richardson

Lord of all, thy creatures see   122
   waiting for their food on thee,
that we may with thanks receive,
   give, herewith thy blessing give.
Fill our mouths with food and praise,
   taste we in the gifts of Grace,
take it as through Jesus given
   eat on earth the Bread of Heaven.
Amen.

Charles Wesley, 1746

God,   123
   isn't your creation wasteful?
Fruits never equal
   the seedlings' abundance.
Springs scatter water.
The sun gives out
   enormous light.
May your bounty teach us
   greatness of heart.
May your magnificence
   stop us being mean.
Seeing you a prodigal
   and open-handed giver,
   let us give unstintingly,
   like God's own.
Amen.

Dom Helder Camara

124   Blessed be the Creator
        and all creative hands
        which plant and harvest,
        pack and haul
        and hand over sustenance
        for our prayer and feasting.
     Blessed be God
        for all, all, all.
     Amen.

Alla Renée Bozarth, alt.

125   The care the eagle gives her young,
        safe in her lofty nest,
     is like the tender love of God
        for us made manifest.
     Amen.

R. Deane Postlethwaite

126   For good food,
        good wine
        and good friends,
     let us thank God,
        and pray that we do not forget
        those less fortunate than ourselves.
     Amen.

Saddlers' Company Grace

O God of our salvation,   127
you are the hope of all the ends of the earth
    and of the farthest seas.
You visit the earth and water it,
    you make it very fruitful.
The waters of heaven brim over their banks,
    providing us with grain,
for so you have prepared the land,
    drenching its furrows,
    settling its ridges,
    softening it with showers,
    and blessing its growth.
from Psalm 65

Bless to us, O God,   128
    the moon above us,
    the sun beyond us,
    the sea about us,
    the earth beneath us,
    the divine within us,
    the friends around us,
    the food before us.
Amen.
WSK

All good gifts around us   129
    are sent from heaven above;
then thank the Lord, O thank the Lord,
    For all his love.
Amen.
Matthias Claudius, 18th century, alt.

130   Bless the agile hands of fruit pickers.
Bless the creativity of cooks.
Bless the refreshing gift of clear water.
Bless those who gather.
Bless the breaking of bread.
Blessed Be!

William John Fitzgerald

131   God of the hungry world
     where everything is a coming
     and going after food
     and emptiness is a sign of the wounds
     we make on one another,
     the inequality of bread the indictment upon us
     of crucifixion of the children of God.

Thank you for a creation where all is food
     and all depend on one another for feeding,
     where sharing and providing
     are paradigms of life,
     and Christ who fed the hungry,
     the parable of holiness ...

God of the hungry world, True Bread, True Wine,
     Food of us, Friend of us,
     Mother and Father, Provider for us,
     Hallowed Be Thy Name.
Amen.

David R. Allan

Bless, O God, before we dine,
    each dish of food,
    each glass of wine;
and make us evermore aware,
    how much, O God,
    we're in your care.
Amen.

Plaisterers' Company Grace, alt.

132

Faithful God,
    let this table
    be a sign of tomorrow's hope
    already here,
when with the world
    which hungers for your justice and peace,
    we shall come together
    to eat our fill.
Amen.

John B. Giuliani, alt.

133

Praise is due to you, O God.
You crown the year with your bounty,
    and your paths overflow with plenty.
The pastures of the wilderness abound with grass,
    and the hills are girded with joy.
The fields are clothed with sheep;
    the valleys are decked with wheat,
they shout and sing together for joy.

from Psalm 65

134

135   Thanks be to God for this food,
the flesh and blood of
rock and water,
earth and sun.
Thanks be to God for this food,
the exacting effort,
the life work of countless beings.
Thanks be to God for
this blessing,
this grace,
this miracle.
Amen.

WSK, based on Edward Espe Brown

136   It is meet before we partake of food to bless
the maker of all things,
and to sing when drinking.

Clement of Alexandria, 2nd century

137   God bless our food;
God bless our drink.
And keep our homes
and ourselves
in your embrace, O God.
Amen.

Brigid's Grace

Gracious God,   138
who has brought to our table
    such a diversity of gifts
      from such a variety of sources;
gather and unite us
    that we too may be a blessing.
Amen.

Anonymous

Brown bread and the Gospel   139
    is good fare.
Praise be to God.

Puritan Saying

You satisfy the hungry heart   140
    with gift of finest wheat.
Come, give to us, O Saving One,
    the bread of life to eat.
Amen.

Omer Westendorf, alt.

Make a joyful noise to God, all the earth;   141
    sing to the honour of God's name;
How awesome are God's deeds!
Come and see what God has done,
    work that is wonderful
      to all earth's children.

from Psalm 66

142 God of mystery and wonder:
  at this and every table
  you dissolve the distance between
  the ordinary and the holy;
 you break the barrier separating
  the common and the sacred.
 We thank you for this thin place,
  this holy space,
  this well of grace.
 Amen.
 WSK

143 We thank you, God,
  for this, our food,
  for life
  and health
  and every good —
 like manna to our souls is given
  this bread of life,
  from earth and heaven.
 Amen.
 John Cennick, 1741, alt.

144 We praise the One
  who gave the growth,
  with voices full and strong.
 Amen.
 Walker's Southern Harmony, 1835

i thank You God for most this amazing 145
day:for the leaping greenly spirits of trees
and a blue true dream of sky;and for everything
which is natural which is infinite which is yes
E. E. Cummings

In Jesus' name we gather here. 146
    Bless, Lord, our food and be us near.
Give us, we pray, that bread divine
    which grants us ever to be thine.
Amen.
Swedish

God of the feast, 147
    sustain us as we come to this table
        and remember.
Fill us, Bread of Life,
    as we recall those
        who have shared
    the bread of their lives
        with us.
Amen.
Jan L. Richardson

The earth has yielded its harvest, 148
    and you, our God, have blessed us.
May you continue to bless us;
    and may all the ends of the earth revere you.
from Psalm 67

149   Holy Wisdom, Creator Spirit,
thank you for this food,
    and keep us always aware of our humble place
    in your web of life.
Thank you for the countless blessings
    which come through all your plants and animals,
    offering us fullness of life,
    in body and in spirit.
Open us to receive such grace
    with mindfulness and humility,
that we may live with respect in creation,
    and know peace
    with all that lives.
Amen.

WSK

150   *Dominus Jesus,*
sit potus et esus.
(Lord Jesus, be drink and food.)
Amen.

Martin Luther, 16th century

151   The Lord is good to me,
    and so I thank the Lord
for giving me the things I need,
    the sun and the rain and the appleseed.
The Lord is good to me.

And every seed that grows
    will grow into a tree.

And one day soon there'll be apples there,
    for everyone in the world to share.
The Lord is good to me.
Amen.

Johnny Appleseed Grace

Jesus comes to wash our feet.   152
Jesus comes to dry them well.
Jesus comes to pour our wine.
Jesus comes to break our bread.
Jesus comes to make us whole.
Amen.

William John Fitzgerald, alt.

You nourish us with food, O God,   153
    for body and for soul.
May love and service
    be our thanks
    for life that's free and whole.
Amen.

Flora Litt and Wayne Irwin, alt.

For food   154
    in a world where many walk in hunger;
for faith
    in a world where many walk in fear;

for friends
    in a world where many walk alone,
we give you thanks, O God.
Amen.

World Hunger Grace,
Girl Guides of Canada

155   Blessed are you, O God,
        who alone does marvellous things.
Blessed is your glorious name forever.
May the whole earth
    be filled with your glory.

from Psalm 72

156   Like Sarah and Abraham,
        we entertain angels here,
        and your presence, O God,
        brings laughter and hope.
Thanks be to you.
Amen.

WSK

157   Every creature of God is good,
        and nothing is to be refused,
        if it be received
        with thanksgiving.
Thanks be to God.
Amen.

1 Timothy 4.4

Many and great, O God, are your works,   158
    Maker of earth and sky.
Your hands have set the heavens with stars,
    your fingers spread the mountains and plains.
Lo, at your word the waters were formed;
    deep seas obey your voice.

Grant unto us communion with you,
    O star-abiding one.
Come unto us and dwell with us,
    with you are found the gifts of life.
Bless us with life that has no end,
    eternal life with you.
Amen.

Dakota Hymn

Let us be thankful   159
    for whatever light, laughter, food and affection
    may come our way.
And let us be mindful of those
    who are sadly without
    these good and golden things.
Amen.

Welsh

160   With this food,
           you make us strong.
      To you
           our life and love belong.
      Thanks be to you, O God.
      Amen.

Flora Litt and Wayne Irwin, alt.

161   Thank you, God, for rain and sun,
           and all the plants that grow.
      Thank you for our daily food,
           and friends who love us so.
      Amen.

Zimbabwean

162   We give thanks to you, O God;
           we give thanks;
           your name is near.
      People tell of your wondrous deeds.

from Psalm 75

163   Every meal is a holy meal
           graced by the Other.
      Every table is a holy table
           laden with blessings.
      And so this space is made sacred
           by simple things
           and a profound purpose:

Food.
Life.
Amen.
WSK

Mothering Christ, 164
   you took our form,
   offering us your food of light,
grain of my life,
   and grape of love,
   your very body for our peace.
Praise and thanks be to you, our Mother.
Amen.
Julian of Norwich, 14th century,
adapt. Jean Wiebe Janzen

Thank you for the world so sweet. 165
   Thank you for the food we eat.
Thank you for the birds that sing.
   Thank you, God, for everything.
Amen.
Anonymous

To render thanks unto our God 166
   it is a comely thing.
So to your name, O God most high,
   due praise aloud we bring.
Amen.
Scottish Psalter, 1650

167   Thank you for the meal
        before us spread.
    For all those who worked to prepare it,
        for the love that leads us to share it,
    we thank you, God.
    Amen.

Girl Guide Grace

168   May all we say and all we think
        be in harmony with you,
    God within, God beyond me,
        maker of all good things.
    Amen.

Chinook Psalter, alt.

169   I will call to mind your deeds, O God!
        I will remember your wonders of old.
    I will recount all your works
        and ponder the things you have done.

from Psalm 77

170   For good food
        and good friends,
        we thank you, God.
    For laughter
        and love,
        we bless you.

For renewal
   and re-creation
   we praise you.
Amen.
WSK

In fellowship assembled here,   171
   we thank thee, Lord,
   for food and cheer,
and through our Saviour, thy dear Son,
   we pray: 'God bless us, every one.'
Amen.
Dickens Fellowship Grace

Eternal Source of good,   172
we thank You for the numberless gifts
and blessings that fill our days:
   for life itself and its endless variety;
   for all that sustains body and mind;
   for love and friendship;
   for the delights of the senses;
   and for the excellence of Your Torah,
      which deepens our life and enriches
      our days.
Amen.
Jewish

173   Mealtime is here.
The board is spread.
Thanks be to God,
    who gives us bread.
Amen.
Girl Guide Grace

174   Come, Lord Jesus, our guest to be
    and bless these gifts bestowed by thee.
Bless our loved ones everywhere
    and keep them in your loving care.
Amen.
Moravian Grace

175   Jesus, you served the best wine at Cana.
You invited strangers to your banquet.
You sat your friends at table
    and washed their feet
    and told us to do likewise.
We rejoice that you are with us still —
    the space between us, very thin.
As we come to this table,
    call us,
    feed us,
    and send us out,
    that we may serve.
Amen.
William John Fitzgerald, alt.

You have done marvellous things, O God.   176
You command the skies above,
    and open the doors of heaven;
you rain down manna to eat,
    and give the grain of heaven.
Mortals eat the bread of angels;
    you send food in abundance.
from Psalm 78

We thank you, God, for this food,   177
    daily bread of our bodies;
and for your good earth,
    daily bread of creation;
and for our loved ones,
    daily bread of the heart.
Amen.
WSK

God bless our meat,   178
God guide our ways,
God give us grace
our Lord to please.
Amen.
George Bellin,
16th century

My friends, let us give thanks for Wonder.   179
Let us give thanks for the Wonder of Life
    that infuses all things now and forever.

Blessed is the Source of Life, the Fountain of Being,
    the wellspring of goodness, compassion and kindness
    from which we draw to make for justice and peace.
From the creative power of Life
    we derive food and harvest,
From the bounty of the earth
    and the yields of the heavens
    we are sustained and are able to sustain others.
Let us give thanks for the power of the heart
    to sense the holy in the midst of the simple.
We eat not simply to satisfy our own appetites,
    we eat to sustain ourselves
    in the task we have been given.
We eat to nourish the vehicle of giving,
    we eat to sustain our task of world repair,
    our quest for harmony, peace and justice.
We eat and we are revived, and we give thanks
    to the lives that were ended to nourish our own.
May we merit their sacrifice,
    and honour their sparks of holiness
    through our deeds of loving kindness.
We give thanks to the Power that makes for Meeting,
    for our table is a place of friendship.
May we never lose touch
    with the simple joy and wonder
    of sharing a meal.
Amen.

Rabbi Rami M. Shapiro, alt.

180   For all our loved ones gathered here,
       for absent loved ones far and near,

for food to hearten us in eating,
   for wine to gladden us in drinking,
for love, for health, for happiness,
   for joy and faith and hope of peace,
for countless other gifts beside,
   we thank you God,
   this even/morning-tide.
Amen.

Anonymous

Bless to us, O God,   181
   each thing our eyes see;
Bless to us, O God,
   each scent that goes to our nostrils;
Bless to us, O God,
   each taste that passes our lips.
Bless to us, O God,
   these gifts.
Amen.

Celtic

God, we give you thanks.   182
   Around this table
   our strength is revived
   in the struggle.
Make of our feasting
   a thirst for abundant life,
   a deeper hunger for justice and hope.
Amen.

Brazilian

183   'I am your God, the Holy One,
         who brought you out of the land of Egypt.
     Open wide your mouth, and I will fill it.
     You I would feed with the finest of wheat,
         you I would satisfy with honey from the rock.'

from Psalm 81

184   You give us bread for living, O God.
     Save us from
         living for bread.
     Amen.

WSK

185   Give thanks to God with one accord
         for all that is set on this board.
     Amen.

Primer, 1553

186   Thanks to God,
         for the gift of friends in Christ,
         for the church, our house of faith,
         for the gift of wondrous love,
         for the gift of endless grace.
     Thanks to God,
     now and for evermore.
     Amen.

Nobuaki Hanaoka

God bless the food 187
   that here we see,
God bless you
   and God bless me.
Amen.

Anonymous

'Blessed are those who hunger and thirst for 188
   justice:
   they will have their fill.
Blessed are those who show mercy to others:
   they will be shown mercy.'
Bless those who gather.
Bless the breaking of bread.
Blessed Be!

Matthew 5.5–7; William John Fitzgerald

For the food we are about to eat, 189
   and for all that sustains us,
we give thanks to the Creator and Sustainer of life.
Amen.

Contemporary Jewish

Show us your steadfast love, O God. 190
Mercy and faithfulness will meet,
   justice and peace will kiss each other.
Faithfulness will spring up from the ground,
   and righteousness will rain down from the sky.

You, O God, will give what is good,
   and our land will yield its harvest.
from Psalm 85

191   May God be praised
      that all things
      be so good.
      Amen.
      John Donne, 16th century

192   God to enfold us,
      Christ to uphold us,
      Spirit to keep us in heaven's sight;
         now may God grace us,
         heal and embrace us,
         feed us and keep us
         through darkness and light.
      Amen.
      John L. Bell, Iona Community, alt.

193   Loving God,
         in a world where many are lonely,
            we thank you for friendship and community;
         in a world where many are despairing,
            we thank you for hope;
         in a world that many find meaningless,
            we thank you for faith;

in a world where many are hungry,
   we thank you for this food;
through Christ, our Lord.
Amen.

Archbishop Ted Scott, alt.

For all we eat,
   and all we wear,
for daily bread,
   and nightly care,
we thank you God.
Amen.

Anonymous

194

Christ on the hillside — 5,000 fed;
   two small fishes,
   five loaves of bread.
May the blessing of him
   who made the division
rest upon us
   and upon our provision.
Amen.

Anonymous

195

Gracious giver of all good,
   you we thank for rest and food.

196

Grant that all we do or say,
  will in your service be, this day.
Amen.

Anonymous

197   God, you have been our dwelling place
      in every generation.
  Before the mountains were brought forth,
      before earth and world were formed,
      from everlasting to everlasting
      you are God.
  Satisfy us in the morning
      with your steadfast love,
  that we may rejoice and be glad
      all our days.

from Psalm 90

198   Let us lay down our burdens
      in the presence of a generous God,
  who gives us
      wine to gladden the heart
      bread for the journey
      and strength for the morrow.
  Amen.

WSK

199   For good health
      and fair wealth,

good food
   and good fellowship,
God's name be praised.
Amen.
Blacksmiths' Company Grace

Our God, we are your guests,   200
   and 'tis you who keeps this generous table.
We thank you.
Amen.
Isle of Lewis Blessing

Bless this meal, O God, we pray,   201
   and bless us, too, throughout the day.
Keep us safe and close to you,
   and kind in all we say and do.
Amen.
Theresa Mary Grass

Like the disciples on the road to Emmaus,   202
   we pause to break bread together.
May our eyes be opened
   and, in this act of common sharing,
   may we see the Risen Christ in one another.
May we see the Lord of Life in our food,
   our conversation,
   and lives shared in common.
May the blessing
   of the God of peace and love
   rest upon our table.
Amen.
Edward Hays, alt.

71

203   God is great,
           God is good,
           and we thank him for our food.
       Amen.

       White House Grace
       (used by President Jimmy Carter)

204   It is good to give you thanks, O God,
           to sing praises to your name, O Most High,
       to tell of your steadfast love in the morning,
           and your faithfulness during the night.

       from Psalm 92

205   Surround this table.
       Bless this food.
       Sustain these bodies.
       And nourish the life of the earth.
       Amen.

       WSK

206   Bless the sheep for David's sake,
           he herded sheep himself;
       Bless the fish for Peter's sake,
           he netted fish himself;
       Bless the swine for Satan's sake,
           he was once a swine himself.
       Amen.

       Old Galloway Grace

May the blessing
 of the five loaves
 and the two fishes
 be ours also.
May we be counted among the five thousand
 who ate and drank to their fill,
 and yet found enough
 to share beyond.
Amen.

Celtic

207

God bless to us our bread,
 and give bread to all those who are hungry,
 and hunger for justice
 to those who are fed.
Amen.

Argentinian, trans. Iona Community

208

For sun and rain, for fruit and grain,
 for friends we love so dearly,
for gentle moments, kindly hearts,
 we thank you, God, sincerely.
Amen.

Anonymous

209

God is great,
God is good,
 let us give thanks for our food.

210

By your hand
   we are fed.
Thank you, God,
   for daily bread.
Amen.

Anonymous

211   O come, let us sing to God,
      let us make a joyful noise
      to the rock of our salvation.
    Let us come into God's presence
      with thanksgiving,
    let us make a joyful noise to God
      with songs of praise.

from Psalm 95

212   Thanks and praise be to you, O God,
      for all that you have given us:
         food and drink
            for flesh and bone;
         story and song
            for soul and spirit;
         your Word and Wisdom,
            for this life
            and the life to come.
    Thanks and praise be to you, O God,
      for all that you have given us.
    Amen.

WSK

One word's as good as ten —
eat away.
Amen.
St Agnes

213

Tireless guardian on our way,
    Thou hast kept us well this day.
While we thank Thee, we request,
    care continued, pardon, rest.
Amen.
Anonymous

214

Each time we eat
    may we remember God's love.
Amen.
Chinese

215

For this and every daily meal,
    we would speak the praise we feel.
Health and strength we have from thee;
    help us, God, to faithful be.
Amen.
Anonymous

216

Generous and Caring God,
    who gave bread to Moses and Miriam
    and their people
    while they travelled in the desert,

217

come now, and bless these gifts of food
　　which you have given to us
　　for our journey.
May we follow the way of your grace,
　　and the pattern of your good creation,
sharing our lives
　　that we be life to one another.
Amen.

Edward Hays, alt.

218　　Make a joyful noise to God,
　　　　all the earth:
worship God
　　with gladness and joy.
Come before God
　　with laughter,
our Maker
　　to whom we belong.
To the Shepherd
　　who tends us like sheep,
let us raise our voices
　　in songs of thanksgiving and praise.

from Psalm 100

219　　Let us break the bread of freedom
　　　　and drink deep from laughter's cup.
Rejoice for God has blessed us.
Thanks be to God.
Amen.

WSK

Some hae meat and canna eat, 220
   and some hae none that want it;
but we hae meat and we can eat,
   and sae the Lord be thankit.
Amen.

Robert Burns

For these and all your gifts of love, 221
   we give you thanks and praise.
Look down, dear God, from heav'n above
   and bless us all our days.
Amen.

WSK

We thank you, God our Creator, 222
   for all things bright and good;
   for seedtime and the harvest,
   our life, our health, our food.
Amen.

Matthias Claudius, 18th century

The bread we break in your company, O God, 223
   is more than bread.
We thank you for this staff of life,
   this food
    for flesh and spirit.
Amen.

WSK

224   By your hand we all are fed;
        thank you, God,
          for daily bread.
    Amen.
    WSK

225   Give thanks to God;
        bless God's holy name.
    Truly you are good, O God:
        you are always gracious,
        and faithful age after age.
    from Psalm 100

226   With each time
    at every table, O God,
    fill us with such longing for your realm,
        that we may go forth
        to turn our food
        into feasting for all —
    that our worship
        may become a witness
        to your reign on earth.
    Amen.
    WSK and Lillian Perigoe

227   Blessing to God, for ever blest,
        to God the Master of the feast,
    who hath for us a table spread,
        and with his daily bounties fed;

may he with all his gifts impart
   the crown of all — a thankful heart.
Amen.

Charles Wesley, 1746

Bless the fruits of the earth.   **228**
Bless the hands of farmers.
Bless the hands of fishers.
Bless the hands of workers.
Bless the textures and colours of my food.
Bless those who gather.
Bless the breaking of bread.
Blessed Be!

William John Fitzgerald

O God,   **229**
   bless this food,
   those who prepare it,
   and those who now share it.
Amen.

Fred Kimbell Graham

Give us in all our toil and sputter,   **230**
   our daily bread, a bit of butter.
Give us our health, our keep to make,
   and enough to spare for others' sake.
Give us, too, a bit of a song,
   and a tale and a book to help us along.

Give us, O God, a chance to be
    our goodly selves, brave, wise and free,
our goodly best, for ourselves and others,
    till all learn to live as sisters, brothers.
Amen.

B. Loydall, alt.

231   Just to be is a blessing.
       Just to live is holy.
       Amen.

       attrib. Rabbi Abraham Joshua Heschel

232   Bless God, O my soul;
           all that is within me,
           bless God's holy name.
       Bless God, O my soul;
           and forget not all God has done for you.
       Bless God,
           who forgives your sin,
           who heals you in all your infirmities,
           who redeems your life from the grave
               and crowns you with mercy and love,
           who fills your life with good things,
               so that your youth is renewed like the eagle's,
           who works righteousness
               and justice for all who are wronged.

       from Psalm 103

It's not supposed to be this way, O God.   233
Some of us have so much,
    while so many have so little.
How can there be such joy at this table
    and such despair in the world?
In the face of such contradictions,
    keep us mindful
        as well as thankful;
    working
        as well as praying;
    needful
        as well as joyful.
Amen.
WSK

The Spirit of God   234
    is a life that bestows life,
root of world-tree
    and wind in its boughs.
Let all the earth praise her!
Amen.
Hildegard of Bingen, 12th century

Grandfather Great Spirit,   235
    all that we have and are
    has come up out of the ground.
Fill us with the Light.

Give us the strength to understand,
    the eyes to see,
      the hearts to receive,
        and teach us to walk the soft Earth
        as relative to all that live.
Amen.

Sioux Prayer, alt.

236   Thank you for the hands that sow the grain.
Thank you for the hands that fish the sea.
Thank you for the sunshine and the rain.
Thank you for the hands that care for me.
Amen.

Brownie Grace

237   To bless the earth God sends us
      from heaven's abundant store
the waters of the springtime,
      enriching it once more.

The seed by God provided
      is sown o'er hill and plain,
and then come gentle showers
      to bless the springing grain.

God crowns the year with goodness,
      the earth God's mercy fills,
the wilderness is fruitful,
      and joyful are the hills.

With grain the fields are covered,
   the flocks in pastures graze;
all nature joins in singing
   a joyful song of praise.
Amen.

The Psalter (1912)

Mother and God,   238
to you we sing:
   wide is your womb,
   warm is your wing.
In you we live,
   move and are fed
   sweet, flowing milk,
   life-giving bread.
Amen.

Miriam Therese Winter

O God, you showed your ways to Moses,   239
   your deeds to the children of Israel.
You are compassionate and merciful,
   slow to anger and extravagant in love.
As a father has compassion for his children,
   so you have compassion for those who are
      in awe of you.
As a mother comforts her child,
   so you comfort us, O God.

from Psalm 103, Isaiah 66.13

240   God of creation,
       we are blessed by your good earth,
       as by a strong and tender mother.
    God of history,
       we benefit from the work of others,
       as by distant but never-failing friends.
    God of hope,
       we thank you for the promise
       of your presence and guidance —
       as certain as this food will give us strength.
    Amen.
WSK

241   May God give us thankful hearts
    and keep us in friendship
    to our lives' end.
    Amen.
Merchant Taylors' Company Grace

242   For all your goodness, God,
       we give you thanks.
    Thanks for the food we eat,
       and for the friends we meet;
    for each new day we greet,
       we give you thanks.
    Amen.
Traditional American

We return thanks to our Mother, the earth,   243
   which sustains us.
We return thanks to the rivers and streams,
   which supply us with water.
We return thanks to all herbs,
   which furnish medicines for the cure
   of our diseases.
We return thanks to the corn, and to her sisters,
   the beans and squashes,
   which give us life.
We return thanks to the wind,
   which, moving the air,
   has banished diseases.
We return thanks to the moon and stars,
   which have given to us their light
   when the sun was gone.
We return thanks to the sun,
   that has looked upon the earth
   with a beneficent eye.
Lastly, we return thanks to the Great Spirit,
   in whom is embodied all goodness,
   and who directs all things
   for the good of his children.
Amen.

Iroquois

Creator God,   244
   bless this food
   through which you re-create our bodies.
May this time of prayer
   re-create our souls,

and this food shared
   help us to re-create our world.
Amen.

Mount St Mary's Abbey, alt.

245   This day God sends me,
      strength to sustain me,
      might to uphold me,
      wisdom as guide.
Your eyes are watchful,
      your ears are listening,
      your lips are speaking,
      O Friend at my side.
Amen.

attrib. St Patrick, alt.

246   O God, how manifold are your works!
With Wisdom at your side you made them all;
    the earth is full of your creatures.
Yonder is the sea,
    great and wide,
teeming with living things
    both great and small.
All these look to you,
    to give them their food in due season.
What you give them
    they gather up.
When you open your hand,
    you fill them with good things.

from Psalm 104

The blessings of heaven and earth,   247
    sea and sky,
    sun and moon,
    are here at this table.
So let us say,
    Thanks be to God.
Amen.
WSK

For the beauty of the earth,   248
    for the glory of the skies,
for the love which from our birth
    over and around us lies,
God of all, to you we raise
    this our prayer of grateful praise.

For the beauty of each hour,
    of the day and of the night,
hill and vale, and tree and flower,
    sun and moon, and stars of night,
God of all, to you we raise
    this our prayer of grateful praise.

For the joy of human love,
    brother, sister, parent, child,
friends on earth, and friends above,
    for all gentle thoughts and mild,
God of all, to you we raise
    this our prayer of grateful praise.
Amen.
Folliott Sandford Pierpoint, 1864, alt.

249   Thank you, God, for
        blue skies above,
        green grass below,
        good friends beside,
        fine food in front,
        and peace,
        wherever it is found.
    Amen.

Celtic

250   O God, ever generous
        in the nourishment of our bodies,
    nourish our spirits too,
        we pray.
    Amen.

Rita F. Snowden

251   God, we begin this meal by giving thanks to you.
    This food is the gift of your creation.
    Protect that creation from all harm and hatred.
    May we cherish the earth
        and all who partake of its richness.
    May we choose life and peace
        so that we and all your children may live.
    We offer our thanks to you,
        our God of peace,
        through Jesus,
        the Prince of Peace.
    Amen.

SCJ Office of Justice and Peace

Thank you, Creator,   252
    for the blessing
    of food (flowers, family and friends ...).
May this Life we receive
    be honored in us.
Bless those by whose lives
    this Feast comes to us.
And may all who hunger
    in body or soul
    be filled.
Amen.
Alla Renée Bozarth

Give thanks and call on God's holy name.   253
    Make known to all peoples what God has done.
Sing to God, sing praises
    and tell of all God's wonderful deeds.
from Psalm 105

God of nurture and need,   254
    thank you for this food;
    keep us mindful of the needs of others.
God of worship and work,
    thank you for this time;
    inspire us for your work in the world.
God of prayer and politics,
    thank you for feeding our hunger —
    but for justice,
    keep us hungry.
Amen.
WSK

255   O Lord, the merciful and good,
        bless and sanctify our food.
    Grant they to us may wholesome be,
        and make us thankful unto thee.
    Amen.

King's Psalter, 1671

256   All who hunger, gather gladly;
        holy manna is our bread.
    Come from wilderness and wandering.
        Here, in truth, we will be fed.
    You that yearn for days of fullness,
        all around us is our food.
    Taste and see the grace eternal.
        Taste and see that God is good.

Sylvia G. Dunstan

257   Bless our house,
        bless our table,
        bless the whole wide world,
    and teach us to take everything
        gratefully from Your hand.
    Amen.

Danish

Dear Mother God,   258
    your wings are warm around us,
we are enfolded in your love and care,
    blessed in this life,
    your heart-beat's pulse surrounds us,
we give you thanks, for you are always here.
Amen.

Janet Wootton, alt.

Blessed are You,   259
O Lord our God,
Eternal King,
    who feeds the whole world
    with Your goodness,
    with grace,
    with loving kindness,
    and with tender mercy.

You give food to all flesh,
    for Your loving kindness endures forever.
Through Your great goodness,
    food has never failed us.
May it not fail us forever.
Amen.

Jewish

O give thanks, for God is good;   260
    God's love endures forever.
Who can recount your works, O God,

or tell of all your praise?
Blessed be the Holy One,
   from everlasting to everlasting.
And let all the people say, 'Amen.'
from Psalm 106

261   Your blessings come to us
      in infinite measure, O God.
    This blessing of ours
      is but a few words
         spoken over a shared meal.
    How is it that, in your presence,
      ordinary words
         put us in touch with
            extraordinary things?
    We marvel
      at how our grace,
         offered to you,
      becomes
         your Grace
            given to us.
    Praise God!
    Amen.
    WSK

262   Father, we thank Thee for this food,
      for health and strength and all things good.

May others all these blessings share,
   and hearts be grateful everywhere.
Amen.

Anonymous, 18th century

Though our mouths were full of song as the sea,   263
   and our tongues of exultation
   as the multitude of its waves,
   and our lips of praise
   as the wide-extended firmament;
though our eyes shone with light
   like the sun and the moon,
   and our hands were spread forth
   like the eagles of heaven,
   and our feet were swift as hinds,
we should still be unable to thank You
   and bless Your name,
O Lord our God and God
   of our fathers and mothers,
   for one thousandth or one ten-thousandth part
   of the bounties which You have bestowed
   upon our forebears and upon us.
Amen.

Jewish

Bless this meal with a grateful heart.   264
Bless the tired feet of waiters and waitresses.
Bless all dishwashers and cleaners.
Bless all who wash the feet of others.

Bless all who share bread with the hungry.
Bless those who gather.
Bless the breaking of bread.
Blessed Be!

William John Fitzgerald

265   God, food of the poor,
Christ, our bread:
    give us a taste of the tender bread
    from your creation's table —
bread newly taken
    from your heart's oven,
    food that comforts and nourishes us;
a communal loaf that makes us human,
    joined hand in hand,
    working and sharing;
a warm loaf that makes us a family,
    sacrament of your body,
    your wounded and life-giving people.
Amen.

Peruvian Soup Kitchen Grace

266   O God, we know
that this food we are about to share
    has already been blessed by you,
        by those who planted it,
        by those who tended it,
        by those who gathered it,
        by those who prepared it.

So bless us, O God,
that we may taste and know
    its blessedness,
as we feast with one another
    at this table you have prepared.
Amen.
Jan L. Richardson

O give thanks, for God is gracious;   267
    God's steadfast love endures for ever.
Thank you, O God, for your steadfast love,
    for the wonders you do for us.
For you satisfy the thirsty,
    and fill the hungry with good things.
from Psalm 107

God of flesh and spirit,   268
    with this food you bless our bodies,
    with this time you sustain our souls.
Help us, therefore, to hold together
    worship and work,
    prayer and politics,
    nurture and need.
Amen.
WSK

269   Give us this day our daily bread,
         and forgive us our sins,
         as we forgive those
         who sin against us.
     Amen.

Matthew 6.11–12

270   Christ beneath me, Christ above me,
     Christ in quiet, Christ in danger,
     Christ in hearts of all that love me,
     Christ in mouth of friend and stranger.
     Amen.

attrib. St Patrick

271   God, our refuge,
         here we are in this home,
         eating, drinking,
         breathing in the Spirit.
     Now rejoice!
     We are together!
     Thanks be to God!

Celtic

272   I'll praise my Maker while I've breath;
         and when my voice is lost in death,
         praise shall employ my nobler powers.

My days of praise shall ne'er be past,
    while life and thought and being last,
    or immortality endures.
Amen.

Isaac Watts; adapt. John Wesley, 1737, alt.

May we share your table,   273
Hostess of the Feast,
    where in the presence of you and many,
all hunger turns to bread
    and all thirst becomes wine.
Amen.

Jan L. Richardson, alt.

Praise God!   274
I will thank you, O God,
    with my whole heart.
Great are your deeds;
    honour and majesty are your work;
    your righteousness endures forever;
You are gracious and full of compassion.
You give food to all who stand in awe of you,
    and keep your covenant always.

from Psalm 111

The ways of the world are puzzling, O God: 275
    war and peace,
        famine and feast.
Show us when to be restless
    and when to be content,

when to feast
   and when to fast,
for our sake
   and the sake of your world.
Amen.
WSK

276   To eat is heaven.
       Confucius, 6th century BC

277   Be known to us in breaking bread,
       but do not then depart;
     Saviour, abide with us, and spread
       thy table in our heart.
     Amen.
     James Montgomery

278   Give us, O God of the nourishing meal,
       well-being to the body, the frame of the soul.
     Give us, O God of the honey-sweet milk,
       the sap and savour of the fragrant farms.
     Amen.
     Celtic

279   For these and all other mercies
       may we be given thankful hearts.
     Amen.
     Ivy Compton-Burnett

God bless this food;
God bless this day,
   and keep us safe
   in every way.
Amen.
Anonymous

280

Praise God!
Give praise, O servants of God;
   praise the name of the Most High.
Blessed be the name of the Holy One
   from this time on and forever.
From the rising of the sun to its setting,
   the name of God is to be praised.
Who is like our God? —
   raising up the poor,
   lifting up the needy,
   giving them a place among princes.
Praise God!
from Psalm 113

281

For this food
   we give thanks.
For those who will not eat today,
   we pray.
For an end to all forms of hunger,
   in body, mind and spirit,
   we long.
Amen.
WSK

282

283   Lord Jesus,
        be with us in this,
        as in all things,
    for your Name's sake.
    Amen.

attrib. Martin Luther,
16th century

284   I will sing of the well-founded Earth,
        Mother of all, eldest of all beings.
    She feeds all creatures that are in the world,
        all that go upon the goodly land,
        all that are in the paths of the seas,
        and all that fly;
        all these are fed by her store.
    Through you, O Queen, we are blessed
        in our loved ones, and in our harvest,
        and to you we owe our lives.
    Amen.

Homeric Hymn

285   All you big things, bless the Lord
    Mount Kilimanjaro and Lake Victoria
    The Rift Valley and the Serengeti Plain
    Fat baobabs and shady mango trees
    All eucalyptus and tamarind trees
    Bless the Lord
    Praise and extol God for ever and ever.
    All you tiny things, bless the Lord
    Busy black ants and hopping fleas

Wriggling tadpoles and mosquito larvae
Flying locusts and water drops
Pollen dust and tsetse flies
Millet seeds and dried dagaa
Bless the Lord
Praise and extol God for ever and ever.
African Canticle

This simple meal   286
   will happier be
if we, O God,
   remember thee.
Amen.
Anonymous

We bless thee, God,   287
   for this our food,
for life and health
   and every good.
May we,
   more blest than we deserve,
live less for self
   and more to serve.
Amen.
Rotary Grace

288   Not to us, O God, not to us,
        but to your name give glory,
    for the sake of your steadfast love
        and your faithfulness.

from Psalm 115

289   Thanks be to God,
        Giver of breath and bread,
    for the life of the Spirit,
        and the spirit of Life.
    Amen.

WSK

290   All things below,
        all things above,
        are formed of your eternal love.
    Thanks be to you, O God.
    Amen.

Herbert O'Driscoll

291   Blessed be the joy of kinship.
    Blessed be the joy of friendship.
    Blessed be the joy of breaking bread.
    Blessed be the fruits of the fertile earth.
    Blessed be God's 'shalom'.

William John Fitzgerald

292   Lord, bless this food upon our dishes,
        as Thou didst bless the loaves and fishes.

And like the sugar in our tea,
　　may we all be stirred by thee.
Amen.

Newfoundland Grace

Holy One,
may our meals
　　on an earth divided
one day be shared
　　in an earth reunited.
Forgive us
this and every unjust meal,
　　until the whole earth
　　is nourished by your bread.
Amen.

Brazilian

293

Come Lord Jesus, be our guest,
　　and let these gifts to us be blest.
Blessed be God, who is our Bread:
　　may all the world be clothed and fed.
Amen.

Gail Ramshaw

294

Praise the Holy One, all you nations!
　　Extol God, all you peoples!

295

For great is God's steadfast love towards us,
   and the faithfulness of God
   endures forever.
Praise God.
from Psalm 117

296   In the name of the One,
      who set the captive free,
      healed the sick
      and fed the hungry,
    we give you thanks and praise.
    Amen.
    WSK

297   Thou who has given so much to me,
      give one thing more,
    a grateful heart,
      for Christ's sake.
    Amen.
    George Herbert, 17th century

298   Blessed be the Lord God of the Universe,
      by whose goodness we live
      and by whose bounty we eat.
    Amen.
    Jewish

Bread is a lovely thing to eat —   299
   God bless the barley and the wheat.
A lovely thing to breathe is air —
   God bless the sunshine everywhere.
The earth's a lovely place to know —
   God bless the folks that come and go.
Alive's a lovely thing to be —
   Giver of life, we say, bless thee!
Amen.

Anonymous

Gratitude is heaven itself.   300
Amen.

William Blake, 18th century

Us   301
and this,
bless.
Amen.

Quaker

Let Israel now say: 302
   'God's love endures for ever.'
Let the house of Aaron say:
   'God's love endures for ever.'
Let those who stand in awe of God say:
   'God's love endures for ever.'
God's deeds are marvellous in our eyes.

This is the day that God has made,
let us rejoice and be glad in it!
from Psalm 118

303   Life-Giver,
Pain-Bearer,
Love-Maker:
　　for bread
　　　and work
　　　　we thank you;
　　for compassion
　　　and peace
　　　　we pray;
　　for love
　　　and life abundant,
　　　　we long.
Life-Giver,
Pain-Bearer,
Love-Maker,
　　may it be so.
Amen.
WSK and Jim Cotter

304   Let us, with a gladsome mind,
　　Praise the Lord, for He is kind:
all things living He doth feed,
　　His full hand supplies their need.
Amen.
John Milton, 17th century

A hundred thousand 305
Welcomes to everyone!
There is always room for more
coming through the doors.

Sit down angel friends.
Sit down Cana couple.
Sit down Martha and Mary.
Sit down Patrick and Bridget.
Sit down guest and stranger.
Sit down poor and homeless.
Sit down Jesus.

A thin place between the living and the dead.
A thin place between friend and stranger.
A thin place between young and old.
A thin place between home and altar.
A thin place between now and heaven.
Amen.

William John Fitzgerald

Grace before us, 306
    grace beside us,
        grace within us —
all by the grace of God.
Amen.

WSK

We sat to eat our simple spread, 307
    then watched the stranger take the bread;

and, as he said the blessing prayer,
    we knew that someone else was there.
Thanks be to God.
Amen.

John L. Bell and Graham Maule,
Iona Community

308   Around this happy table
    may no evil ever come,
but health and peace and happiness
    make up our daily sum.
Amen.

Anonymous

309   How very good and pleasant it is
    when kindred dwell together in unity!
Thanks be to God.

from Psalm 133

310   We reap, O God, where others sow.
And so we pray for your blessing
    on all who labour
    in field
        and farm
            and factory,

in order that we here may break bread
　　and lift a glass
　　　　in joy and thanksgiving.
Amen.
WSK

Benedictus benedicat.   311
(Let the blessed bless.)
Amen.
British Legal Society Grace

The food comes from the baker,   312
　　the drink comes from the vine,
the words come from the Saviour,
　　'I will meet you in bread and wine.'
Thanks be to God.
Amen.
John L. Bell and Graham Maule,
Iona Community

Help us to keep our ears to the earth,   313
　　and our eyes in the stars.
Amen.
Steve Myrvang

Give us grace, O God,   314
　　to be ever thankful for your providence,

with hearts always ready to provide
  for the needs of others.
Amen.

St Francis of Assisi

315   God's grace is the only grace
         and all grace is the grace of God.
       Thanks be to God.

       Coventry Patmore

316   O God, you have searched me and known me.
       You know when I sit down and when I rise up;
          you discern my thoughts from afar.
       Before a word is on my tongue,
          you know it, O God, completely.
       It was you who formed my inward parts;
          you fashioned me in my mother's womb.
       I praise you, for I am fearfully, wonderfully made.
          Wondrous are your works; that I know very well.
       How deep your designs are to me, O God!
          How great their number!
       I try to count them
          but they are more than the sand.

       from Psalm 139

317   Heaven is here,
       and earth,
          and the space is thin between them.

The gifts of soil and sea
and the very bread of heaven
    meet at this table
    and are held in our hands.
Let joy and thanksgiving
    mark the meal.
Amen.

John L. Bell, Iona Community, alt.

Gracious, O God, are thy gifts of food and drink;   318
    gracious, too, this place where we enjoy them.
Let gratitude fill our hearts with joy,
    and equity the land with justice.
Amen.

Judge's Grace

Since the world was young,   319
    there's a song that's been sung
    of a promise coming true:
hungry folk will eat,
    long-lost friends will meet
    and God will make all things new.
May it be so.
Amen.

John L. Bell and Graham Maule,
Iona Community, alt.

320   Even though we walk through the darkest valley,
        we fear no evil,
        for God is with us.
    God prepares a table before us;
        the oil of gladness is poured out,
        our cup overflows,
        goodness and mercy follows us always.
    Thanks be to God.
    Amen.

23rd Psalm Grace

321   Source and Sustainer of life,
        as we come to this table,
        we offer thanks
        for the wonder of your love:
    Thanks be to you, O God.
    In companionship with all creatures,
        we are one in gratitude
        for the gift and mystery of life,
        and one in longing for a world reborn.
    May this food strengthen us to that end.
    May it be so, O God.
    Amen.

Peter Wyatt, alt.

322   O God, how lovely it is to be your guest,
        to taste of your fruit
        and be blessed by your hand.

For the promise of dawn's awakening,
   and the peace of evening rest —
     and in between,
     the sustenance of food and friends —
   we give you praise.
Glory to you for the feast that is life.
Amen.
Gregory Petrov, alt.

Every day we will bless you   **323**
   and praise your name forever.
O God, you are great and highly to be praised;
   your greatness is beyond all measure.
from Psalm 145

Ever-present God,   **324**
   you come to us in the stranger's guise
   and are known in every breaking of bread.
Come, sit among us, we pray
   as both friend and stranger.
Remind us of your presence
   on the road which brought us here;
reassure us of your guidance
   on the path that lies ahead;
and show us your way
   in the sharing of our bread.
Amen.
WSK

Without your sunshine and your rain   **325**
   we would not have your golden grain.

Without your love, we'd not be fed:
    we thank you for our daily bread.
Amen.

Traditional Gaelic

326   Food enough that all may feed,
        grace enough for each one's need.
Even as we praise you, singing,
    you come bringing
    gifts at every day's beginning.
Thanks be to you, O God.
Thanks be to you.
Amen.

Hungarian

327   God, we thank you for this food,
        for rest and home and all things good.
For wind and rain and sun above,
    and, most of all, for those we love.
Amen.

Anonymous

328   Blessed be the taste of food.
Blessed be the staff of life.
Blessed be the abundance of the market.
Blessed be the freedom of meal-making.
Bless those who gather.
Bless the breaking of bread.
Blessed Be!

William John Fitzgerald

As Christ breaks bread,
   and bids us share,
      each proud division ends.
The love that made us,
   makes us one,
      and strangers now are friends.

The Spirit of the risen Christ,
   unseen, but ever near,
is in such friendship
   better known,
     alive among us here.
Amen.
Brian Wren

329

O God, you are gracious and merciful,
   slow to anger
   and abounding in steadfast love.
Your compassion is over all.
from Psalm 145

330

Blessing
and laughter
and love
   be with us —
in hands held,
in food shared,
in nurture known.
Amen.
WSK

331

332   We praise you for the sun,
         the golden shining sun,
that gives us healing, strength and joy.
      We praise you for the sun.

We praise you for the rain,
      the softly falling rain,
that gives us healing, strength and joy.
      We praise you for the rain.

We praise you for your love,
      your patient, endless love,
that gives us healing, strength and love.
      We praise you for your love.
Amen.

Alice Muriel Pullen

333   Wind from the west, fish and bread.
Wind from the north, cold and flaying.
Wind from the east, snow on the hills.
Wind from the south, fruit on trees.
Blessed be the winds of God.
Amen.

Scottish

334   Thank you, God, for bread and milk,
      and other things so good.

And thank you, God, for those who help
   to grow and cook our food.
Amen.

Anonymous

Blessed Lord, we pray thee   335
   to be present at our table,
hallowing thy gifts to our use;
   that eating to satisfy our needs
we may remember those who lack.
Amen.

St Francis of Assisi

The flying birds and swimming fish,   336
   the sea and sky and mountains tall —
the earth serves up a tasty dish,
   O God, we thank you for them all.
Amen.

Anonymous

The eyes of all look to you,   337
   and you give them their food in due season.
You open your hand,
   satisfying the desire of every living thing.
You are just in all your ways,
   and kind in all your doings.

from Psalm 145

338   We gather at this table, O God,
        remembering your blessings.
We join hands,
        feeling the touch of your presence.
We break bread together,
        offering thanks for what has been given.
And we lift a glass,
        and long for what is yet to be.
Amen.

WSK

339   Draw us in the Spirit's tether,
        for when humbly in your name
two or three are met together,
        you are in the midst of them.

All our meals and all our living
        make as sacraments of you,
that by caring, helping, giving,
        we may be disciples true.
Amen.

Percy Dearmer, 1931

340   I bow down to that Goddess
        who lives within everybody
        in the form of Hunger.
Amen.

Indian, 12th century

Eat your bread with joy   341
    and drink with a merry heart,
    for God has blessed us.
Amen.
Mount St Mary's Abbey, alt.

Thank you for the wind and rain   342
    and sun and pleasant weather;
and thank you now for this our food
    and that we are together.
Amen.
Mennonite Blessing

Food —   343
God's love made edible.
Praise be.
Amen.
Brother Thomas, alt.

Praise God, O my soul!   344
    As long as I live, I will praise God.
Happy are those whose help is the God of Jacob,
    whose hope is the Holy One,
who made heaven and earth,
    the sea, and all that is in them;
who keeps faith forever;
who gives justice to the oppressed,
who gives food to the hungry.
from Psalm 146

345   For the greening of trees
          and the gentling of friends,
             we thank you, God.
For the wind in the meadow
        and the warmth in this house,
           we thank you, God.
We thank you, and know
      that with hands to hold
         around this groaning board,
      there is hope for the morrow
        and all shall be well.
Yes, all shall be well.
Amen.

WSK, based on Kate McIlhagga,
Iona Community

346   For all the glory of the way,
        for thy protection, night and day,
for roof-tree, fire, and bed and board,
        for friends and home, we thank you, Lord.
Amen.

Wayfarer's Grace

May God bless our meal 347
   and grant us a compassionate
   and understanding heart
   towards one another.
Amen.

Mount St Mary's Abbey, alt.

We thank you 348
   for our daily bread.
Let also, God,
   our souls be fed.
O Bread of Life,
   from day to day
sustain us on
   our homeward way.
Amen.

The Eckhardt family

Bless us and each of our families. 349
Bless this food we eat.
And may we be a blessing
   to all that we meet.
Amen.

Christian Renewal Center,
Silverton, Oregon

350   *Everyone at the table raises their plates for*
            a moment of silence, ending with:
        Thanks be to God.
        Anonymous

351   How good it is
                to give praises to God,
            how pleasant and fitting
                to laud the Most High.
            You determine the number of the stars,
                and give to all of them their names.
            You cover the sky with clouds,
                prepare rain for the earth,
                and make the hills green with grass.
            You give the cattle their food,
                and feed the young ravens when they cry.
            You heal the broken-hearted,
                and bind up their wounds.
            How good it is
                to give praises to you, O God.
            from Psalm 147

352   Come, Spirit of Justice,
                and bless our hands
            to break bread with our neighbours,
                and share life in the land.
            Amen.
            WSK

The Sacred Three be blessing thee,
    this table and its store.
The Sacred Three be blessing
    all your loved ones evermore.
Amen.

Stranger's Grace, alt.

353

There's a wideness in God's mercy
    like the wideness of the sea;
there's a kindness in God's justice
    which is more than liberty.

For the love of God is broader
    than the measures of the mind,
and the heart of the Eternal
    is most wonderfully kind.
Amen.

Frederick William Faber, 1854, alt.

354

Come, Spirit of God,
    and make this food sweet!
Give strength to our hands,
    and direct our feet.

WSK

355

The blessing of Columba upon this house —
    on man and woman, on spouse and child,
    on old and young, on maiden and youth —

356

with plenty of food and plenty of drink,
   with plenty of beds and plenty of ale,
   with many riches and much cheer,
   with many kin and length of life —
ever upon it.
Amen.

Scottish

357   O God, you are
   the giver of every good and perfect gift.
We are aware of how easily we take
   and how often we grudgingly give.
Give us the gift of grateful hearts,
   that we may want to share freely with others
   all you have given us.
Amen.

Society of St Paul, Diocese of San Diego

358   Praise God from the heavens;
   give praise in the heights!
Give praise, all you angels;
   praise God, all you hosts!
Praise God, sun and moon;
   give praise, stars and lights!
Praise God from the earth,
   great sea creatures and ocean depths,
lightning and hail, snow and frost,
   gales that obey God's decree,
all mountains and hills,
   all fruit trees and cedars,

wild animals and cattle,
    creatures winged and earth-bound,
sovereigns who rule earth and its people,
    all who govern and judge this world,
young men and women alike,
    old people and children together!
Let all things praise the name of God,
    the name above every other,
whose splendour covers heaven and earth.

from Psalm 148

Blest and blessing God,   359
    bless our bodies with your bounty,
    our lives with your love,
    and our world with your work.
Amen.

WSK

Give us food,   360
    enough for health and well-being.
Give us grace and strength
    to forbear and to persevere.
Give us courage and gaiety
    and the quiet mind.
Spare to us our friends,
    soften to us our enemies.
Amen.

Robert Louis Stevenson, alt.

361   O you who clothe the lilies
        and feed the birds of the air,
who leads the lambs to pasture,
        and the hart to the water's side,
who has multiplied loaves and fishes,
        and changed the water into wine —
come to our table
        as giver and guest to dine.
Amen.

Stephen Doyle, OFM

362   Lord Jesus, be our holy guest,
        our morning prayer,
        our evening rest,
and with this daily food impart
        thy love and grace
        to every heart.
Amen.

President D. D. Eisenhower's Grace

363   The Sacred Three
        my fortress be,
        encircling me.
Come and be round
        my hearth,
        my home.
Amen.

Hebridean Chant

Bless our hearts   364
    to hear in the
    breaking of bread
the song of the universe.
Amen.
John B. Giuliani

Praise God in the sanctuary!   365
    Praise God in the holy temple!
Praise God for bountiful mercies!
    Praise God who meets all needs!
Praise God wherever you are!
    Let everything that breathes praise God!
from Psalm 150

Notes and Acknowledgements

Grateful acknowledgement is made by the author to the following individuals and publishers for use of their material. Every effort has been made to trace the owner(s) and/or administrator(s) of each copyright. Listed below, according to prayer number, are those items for which copyright ownership applies. Material in the public domain and items which are traditional, of anonymous authorship or of unknown origin, are not included in this list.

1   *Voices United* (Toronto: United Church Publishing House, 1996), p. 732. Used with permission. The psalms in *A Year of Grace* are based upon the translation found in *Voices United*, with adaptations based on the New Revised Standard Version (NRSV) of the Bible. The New Revised Standard Version of the Bible is copyright © 1989 by the Division of Christian Education of the National Council of Churches of Christ in the USA. Used by permission. All rights reserved.

2   William S. Kervin.

3   Sylvia G. Dunstan, from 'All Who Hunger, Gather Gladly', *In Search of Hope and Grace* © 1991 GIA Publications, Inc., Chicago, Illinois. All rights reserved. Used with permission.

4   J. S. Woodsworth, attributed. Contributed by Marilyn Legge, Emmanuel College, Toronto.

5   From Sister Mary Teresa, OP, excerpts from *Prayers at Mealtime*, copyright © 1972 by the Missionary Society of St Paul the Apostle in the State of New York, Paulist Press, Inc., New York/Mahwah, NJ. Used with permission. www.paulist-press.com

8   *Voices United*, pp. 732–3.

9   William S. Kervin.

10 Scottish Psalter, 1650. Lavon Baylor, 'God Is My Shepherd' from *The New Century Hymnal* (Cleveland: The Pilgrim Press, 1995), 479. Word adaptations copyright © 1992 The Pilgrim Press. Used by permission.

12 Betty Lynn Schwab. Used with permission.

14   Rita F. Snowden, *More Prayers for Women*. William Collins Sons & Co. Ltd. (Fontana) © 1975. Used with permission of HarperCollins Publishers Ltd, London.

15   *Voices United*, p. 734.

16   William S. Kervin, based on *A Wee Worship Book (Fourth Incarnation)* (Glasgow: Wild Goose Publications, 1999), pp. 16–17.

18   © 1970 Walter Farquharson. Used with permission.

19   Jeffrey W. Rowthorn, 'Creating God Your Fingers', copyright © 1978 Hope Publishing Co. Administered by Copycare, PO Box 77, Hailsham BN27 3EF, UK, music@copycare.com. Used by permission.

20   From William John Fitzgerald, *A Contemporary Celtic Prayer Book* (Chicago: ACTA, 1998), p. 40. Used with permission.

21   Diane Taylor and Ken Powers, alt. © 1991, Prairie Rose Publications. Used with permission.

22   *Voices United*, p. 738.

23   William S. Kervin.

24   Fred Pratt Green. Reproduced by permission of Stainer & Bell Ltd and Hope Publishing Co. (United States and Canada).

25   Based on words from Alexander Carmichael, *Carmina Gadelica: Hymns and Incantations Collected in the Highlands and Islands of Scotland in the Last Century* (Edinburgh: Floris Books, 1992, 1994).

26   From a eucharistic prayer by Gail Ramshaw. Used with permission.

28   Based on a prayer from Mount St Mary's Abbey, Wrentham, Mass. Used with permission.

29   *Voices United*, p. 744.

30   William S. Kervin.

31   From verse 3 of the hymn 'Mothering God, You Gave Me Birth', by Jean Wiebe Janzen, based on the words of Julian of Norwich, *c.* 1400. Used with permission.

32   Anonymous grace. Translated by William S. Kervin.

33   Jan L. Richardson, *Sacred Journeys: A Woman's Book of Daily Prayer*. Copyright 1995 by Jan L. Richardson. Used by permission of Upper Room Books.

36   *Voices United*, p. 749.

37   William S. Kervin.

38   Based on the Woolmen's Company Grace, the Worshipful Company of Woolmen, Buckinghamshire, UK. Used with permission.

40   Wind Daughter, Medicine Chief of the Bear Tribe, Spokane, Washington. Used with permission.

129

41   Abbey of New Clairvaux, alt., Vina, California. Used with permission.

43   *Voices United*, p. 750.

44   William S. Kervin.

46   Contributed by Marilyn Legge and Michael Bourgeois. The original version was seen in the Methodist chapel in Hawkshead, England.

47   From a eucharistic prayer by Gail Ramshaw. Used with permission.

49   Carter Heyward, *Our Passion for Justice: Images of Power, Sexuality, and Liberation* (The Pilgrim Press: Cleveland, 1984), pp. 50–1. Copyright © 1984 The Pilgrim Press. Used by permission.

50   *Voices United*, p. 758.

51   William S. Kervin.

52   Based on the words of Julian of Norwich, *c.* 1400, adapted by Jean Wiebe Janzen. Used with permission.

53   Jim Strathdee, verse 2 of 'God, We Praise You for the Morning', © 1985 Desert Flower Music. Used with permission.

54   Jan L. Richardson, *Sacred Journeys: A Woman's Book of Daily Prayer*. Copyright 1995 by Jan L. Richardson. Used by permission of Upper Room Books.

56   From Beverly Wildung Harrison. The story goes that a Communist Party organizer and an Episcopal bishop were finally able to agree on these words at table as a suitable grace.

57   *Voices United*, p. 761.

58   William S. Kervin.

60   Sylvia G. Dunstan, from 'All Who Hunger, Gather Gladly', *In Search of Hope and Grace* © 1991 GIA Publications, Inc., Chicago, Illinois. All rights reserved. Used with permission.

63   Reprinted by permission from *Thank You for This Food: Action Prayers, Songs, and Blessings for Mealtime* by Debbie Trafton O'Neal. Copyright © 1994 Augsburg Fortress.

64   *Voices United*, p. 762.

65   William S. Kervin.

69   Used with permission of Guiding, UK.

70   Congregation of Abraxas, a Unitarian Congregation for Liturgical Renewal.

71   *Voices United*, p. 762.

72   William S. Kervin and Lillian Perigoe. Used with permission.

74   Traditional Cameroon (Mungaka). English translation Gerald R. Hobbs. © 1987 *Songs for a Gospel People* published by Wood Lake Books, Kelowna, BC, Canada. Used by permission.

75   From William John Fitzgerald, *A Contemporary Celtic Prayer*

Book (Chicago: ACTA, 1998), p. 19. Used with permission.

78   *Voices United*, p. 764.

79   William S. Kervin.

82   'Gather Us In' (call to worship), from *A Wee Worship Book (Fourth Incarnation)* (Glasgow: Wild Goose Publications, 1999), words by John L. Bell (excerpt), copyright © 1999 Wild Goose Resource Group, Iona Community, Glasgow, G3 2DH. Scotland.

83   Reprinted by permission from *Thank You for This Food: Action Prayers, Songs, and Blessings for Mealtime* by Debbie Trafton O'Neal. Copyright © 1994 Augsburg Fortress.

84   William N. Richards and James Richardson, Kenya. Uzima Press. Used with permission.

85   *Voices United*, pp. 768–9.

86   William S. Kervin.

88   Kathy Galloway, 'Lord Jesus, It's Good to Know' from *The Pattern of Our Days*, edited by Kathy Galloway. *The Pattern of Our Days* © 1996 The Iona Community, published by Wild Goose Publications, Glasgow G2 3DH, Scotland. Used with permission.

89   Julia Esquivel, 'The Lord's Prayer from Guatemala', *Threatened with Resurrection*, copyright © 1994 by Brethren Press. Used with permission.

92   *Voices United*, p. 777.

93   William S. Kervin, based on 'Bless to Us, O God' by Kate McIlhagga from *The Pattern of Our Days*, edited by Kathy Galloway. *The Pattern of Our Days* © 1996 The Iona Community, published by Wild Goose Publications, Glasgow G2 3DH, Scotland. Used with permission.

94   Miller's Grace; also known as the Baker's Grace.

96   Based on Proverbs 8.1–3, 5–6, and an adaption by Pamela Ann Moeller. Used with permission.

99   *Voices United*, p. 778.

100   William S. Kervin, based on 'May the Maker's Blessing Be Yours' by Ruth Burgess from *The Pattern of Our Days*, edited by Kathy Galloway. *The Pattern of Our Days* © 1996 The Iona Community, published by Wild Goose Publications, Glasgow G2 3DH, Scotland. Used with permission.

101   Sailors' Grace, heard by William S. Kervin in Nova Scotia, Canada.

106   NRSV.

107   William S. Kervin, based on an anonymous source.

109   William S. Kervin.

110   Holden Village Ecumenical Christian Retreat Center, Chelan,

Washington. Used with permission.

112   William S. Kervin and Janet Cawley. Used with permission.

113   NRSV.

114   William S. Kervin.

115   Verse 1 of 'This Day God Gives Me', attributed to St Patrick, *c.* 370–460, adapt. © 1969, James Quinn, SJ, Selah Publishing Co. Used with permission.

116   William S. Kervin, based on William John Fitzgerald, *A Contemporary Celtic Prayer Book* (Chicago: ACTA, 1998), pp. 26–7. Used with permission.

118   Verses 1, 4, 3 of 'God of the Sparrow', by Jaroslav J. Vajda, © 1984 Concordia Publishing House. Used with permission.

121   William S. Kervin, based on Jan L. Richardson, *Sacred Journeys: A Woman's Book of Daily Prayer* (Nashville: Upper Room Books, 1995), p. 109.

123   Dom Helder Camara, Brazil, in *The Desert is Fertile*. English translation, Maryknoll, NY: Orbis Books, 1974, 1982. Originally published by Desclée de Brouwer, Paris. Used with permission of the Council of Curators, *Istituto Dom Helder Camara*.

124   Alla Renée Bozarth, from 'The Blessing of the Stewpot', in *Moving to the Edge of the World: A Poetry Trilogy* © iUniverse.com, 2000. Used with permission.

125   Verse 1 of 'The Care the Eagle Gives Her Young', by R. Deane Postlethwaite, © Marjean Postlethwaite. Used with permission.

126   Saddlers' Company Grace, the Worshipful Company of Saddlers, London, UK. Used with permission.

127   *Voices United*, p. 782.

128   William S. Kervin, based on *A Wee Worship Book* (Wild Goose Publications, 1999), copyright © 1999 Wild Goose Resource Group, Iona Community, Glasgow G3 2DH, Scotland.

130   William John Fitzgerald, *A Contemporary Celtic Prayer Book* (Chicago: ACTA, 1998), pp. 49–50. Used with permission.

131   From 'God of the Hungry World', by David R. Allan, *Crosswalks: Prayers from a City Church* (Toronto: United Church Publishing House, 1993), pp. 141–2. Reprinted with permission.

132   Plaisterers' Company Grace, the Worshipful Company of Plaisterers, London, UK. Used with permission.

133   John B. Giuliani, alt. The Benedictine Grange, Redding, Connecticut. Used with permission.

134   *Voices United*, p. 782.

135   William S. Kervin, based on words by Edward Espe Brown, in Elizabeth Roberts and Elias Amidon, *Earth Prayers from around*

the World. 365 Prayers, Poems and Invocations for Honoring the Earth (San Francisco: HarperCollins, 1991), p. 346.

140   Refrain from 'You Satisfy the Hungry Heart', by Omer Westendorf, © 1976 Archdiocese of Philadelphia. Used with permission.

142   William S. Kervin.

145   E. E. Cummings. 'i thank You God for most this amazing' is reprinted from *Complete Poems 1904–1962*, by E. E. Cummings, edited by George J. Firmage, by permission of W. W. Norton & Company. Copyright © 1991 by the Trustees for the E. E. Cummings Trust and George James Firmage.

146   Sven Evander, alt. Used with permission.

147   Jan L. Richardson, *Sacred Journeys: A Woman's Book of Daily Prayer*. Copyright 1995 by Jan L. Richardson. Used by permission of Upper Room Books.

148   *Voices United*, p. 786.

149   William S. Kervin, based on an anonymous source. The phrase 'live with respect in creation' is from an affirmation of faith of The United Church of Canada, also known as 'A New Creed'.

152   William John Fitzgerald, *A Contemporary Celtic Prayer Book* (Chicago: ACTA, 1998), pp. 62–3. Used with permission.

153   Flora Litt and Wayne Irwin, alt. Used with permission.

154   Attrib. Girl Guide World Hunger Grace, Hunger Task Force, Anglican Church, Diocese of Huron, Canada. Used with permission.

155   William S. Kervin.

157   NRSV.

158   Dakota hymn, Joseph R. Renville 1824; paraphrased Philip Frazier 1929, alt., © South Dakota Conference, United Church of Christ. Used with permission.

159   Based on an anonymous Welsh source.

160   Flora Litt and Wayne Irwin, alt. Used with permission.

161   Based on an anonymous Zimbabwean source.

162   NRSV.

163   William S. Kervin.

164   From verse 2 of the hymn 'Mothering God, You Gave Me Birth', by Jean Wiebe Janzen, based on the words of Julian of Norwich, *c.* 1400. Used with permission.

167   Used with permission of Guiding, UK.

169   *Voices United*, p. 791.

170   William S. Kervin.

171   The Dickens Fellowship, London. Used with permission.

172   *Gates of Prayer. The New Union Prayerbook* (New York: Central Conference of American Rabbis, 1975), © 1975,

Central Conference of American Rabbis, New York. Used with permission.

173 Used with permission of Guiding, UK.

175 Based on William John Fitzgerald, *A Contemporary Celtic Prayer Book* (Chicago: ACTA, 1998), p. 58. Used with permission.

176 NRSV.

177 William S. Kervin, inspired by Ralph Waldo Emerson's phrase, 'the sky is the daily bread of the eyes'.

179 Rabbi Rami M. Shapiro. Used with permission.

181 Based on words from Alexander Carmichael, *Carmina Gadelica: Hymns and Incantations Collected in the Highlands and Islands of Scotland in the Last Century* (Edinburgh: Floris Books, 1992, 1994).

182 From Jaci C. Maraschin, *New Gestures, New Gazes: Guide for Reading and Celebrating the Gospel of Luke*, edited by Nancy Pereira and Ernesto Cardoso, © 1993 Institute for Religious Studies, Rio de Janeiro, Brazil. Used with permission.

183 *Voices United*, p. 797.

184 William S. Kervin, inspired by Ralph Waldo Emerson's lines, 'He thought it happier to be dead, / To die for Beauty, than live for bread.'

186 From verse 2 of the hymn 'Praise to God', © 1980 Nobuaki Hanaoka. Used with permission.

188 NRSV and William John Fitzgerald, *A Contemporary Celtic Prayer Book* (Chicago: ACTA, 1998), pp. 73–4. Used with permission.

190 *Voices United*, p. 802.

192 From *Love and Anger* (Glasgow: Wild Goose Publications, 1997), words by John L. Bell, copyright © 1997 Wild Goose Resource Group, Iona Community, Glasgow G3 2DH, Scotland. Text altered by permission.

193 Archbishop Ted Scott, alt., Primates' Task Force on World Hunger. Used with permission.

197 *Voices United*, p. 803.

198 William S. Kervin, based on *The Pattern of Our Days,* edited by Kathy Galloway (Glasgow: Wild Goose Publications, 1996), p. 160.

199 Herbert Payne, Prime Warden of the Worshipful Company of Blacksmiths, 1954, London, UK. Used with permission.

201 Theresa Mary Grass. Reprinted with permission. Excerpted from *Graces: Prayers and Poems for Everyday Meals and Special Occasions* by June Cotner (HarperSanFrancisco © 1994).

202 Edward M. Hays, alt., *Prayers for the Domestic Church* (Easton, Kansas: Forest of Peace Books, 1980), p. 111. Used with permission.

204 *Voices United*, p. 810.

205 William S. Kervin, with a line from a eucharistic prayer by Gail Ramshaw. Used with permission.

208 'God Bless to Us Our Bread', from *Love and Anger* (Glasgow: Wild Goose Publications, 1997), Argentinian source unknown.

211 *Voices United*, p. 814.

212 William S. Kervin.

217 Edward M. Hays, alt., *Prayers for the Domestic Church* (Easton, Kansas: Forest of Peace Books, 1980), p. 109. Used with permission.

218 *Voices United*, p. 824.

219 William S. Kervin, based on lines from *Celebrate God's Presence: A Book of Services for The United Church of Canada* (Toronto: The United Church Publishing House, 2000), p. 268.

221 William S. Kervin, based on an anonymous source.

223 William S. Kervin, inspired by Conrad Aiken's line, 'And bread I broke with you was more than bread'.

224 William S. Kervin.

225 *Voices United*, p. 824.

226 William S. Kervin and Lillian Perigoe. Used with permission.

228 William John Fitzgerald, *A Contemporary Celtic Prayer Book* (Chicago: ACTA, 1998), pp. 27–8. Used with permission.

229 Fred Kimbell Graham. Used with permission.

230 B. Loydall, alt. From *A Book of Graces*, compiled by Carolyn Martin (London: Hodder & Stoughton, 1980, 1986). Used with permission.

231 Attributed to Rabbi Abraham Joshua Heschel. Source unknown.

232 *Voices United*, p. 824.

233 William S. Kervin.

234 Adapted from Saint Hildegard of Bingen, Barbara Newman (ed. and trans.): *Symphonia: A Critical Edition of the* Symphonia Armonie Celestium Revelationum *(Symphony of the Harmony of Celestial Revelations)*, Second Edition. Copyright © 1988, 1998 by Cornell University. Used by permission of the publisher, Cornell University Press.

236 Used with permission of Guiding, UK.

238 The refrain of the hymn 'Mother and God' by Miriam Therese Winter, copyright Medical Mission Sisters 1987. Used with permission.

239 *Voices United*, p. 825.

240 William S. Kervin.

241   The Worshipful Company of Merchant Taylors, London, UK. Used with permission.

245   Verse 2 of 'This Day God Gives Me', attributed to St Patrick, *c.* 370–460, adapt. © 1969, James Quinn, SJ. Used by permission of Selah Publishing Co. Inc., North American Agent.

246   NRSV.

247   William S. Kervin.

250   Rita F. Snowden, *More Prayers for Women*. William Collins Sons & Co. Ltd. (Fontana) © 1975. Used with permission of HarperCollins Publishers Ltd, London.

251   SCJ Office of Justice and Peace, Priests of the Sacred Heart, Hales Corners, Wisconsin. Used with permission.

252   Alla Renée Bozarth. Used with permission.

253   *Voices United*, p. 828.

254   William S. Kervin.

256   Sylvia G. Dunstan, from 'All Who Hunger, Gather Gladly', *In Search of Hope and Grace*, © 1991 GIA Publications, Inc., Chicago, Illinois. All rights reserved. Used with permission.

257   Poul-Erik Fabricius, alt. Used with permission.

258   From verse 1 of the hymn 'Dear Mother God', by Janet Wootton, alt. Reproduced by permission of Stainer & Bell Ltd and Hope Publishing Co. (United States and Canada).

259   A Hebrew *Berakhah* (Blessing). From *One Hundred Graces* by Marcia Kelly and Jack Kelly, copyright © 1992 by Marcia Kelly and Jack Kelly. Foreword copyright © 1992 by Toinette Lippe. Used by permission of Bell Tower, a division of Random House, Inc.

260   *Voices United*, p. 830.

261   William S. Kervin.

264   William John Fitzgerald, *A Contemporary Celtic Prayer Book* (Chicago: ACTA, 1998), pp. 60–1. Used with permission.

265   From workers in community soup kitchens in the shanty towns of Lima, Peru: one of the 'Psalms for Life and Peace' that first appeared in the journal *Paginas*: reprinted in *Latinamerica Press* (5 November 1987). Used with permission of SPCK.

266   Jan L. Richardson, *Sacred Journeys: A Woman's Book of Daily Prayer*. Copyright 1995 by Jan L. Richardson. Used by permission of Upper Room Books.

267   *Voices United*, p. 831.

268   William S. Kervin.

269   NRSV.

271   Based on *Celtic Daily Prayer* (London: HarperCollins, 2000), p. 300.

273   Jan L. Richardson, *Sacred Journeys: A Woman's Book of Daily*

Prayer. Copyright 1995 by Jan L. Richardson. Used by permission of Upper Room Books.

274   *Voices United*, p. 833.

275   William S. Kervin.

278   Based on words from Alexander Carmichael, *Carmina Gadelica: Hymns and Incantations Collected in the Highlands and Islands of Scotland in the Last Century* (Edinburgh: Floris Books, 1992, 1994).

279   Ivy Compton-Burnett, *Pastors and Masters* (London: Gollancz, 1972). © Orion Publishing Group.

281   NRSV.

282   William S. Kervin.

287   Rotary Grace. Used with permission.

288   NRSV.

289   William S. Kervin, inspired by Gerard Manley Hopkins' phrase 'giver of breath and bread'.

290   The refrain from the hymn 'O God, Beyond All Face and Form', by Herbert O'Driscoll, © 1993, Herbert O'Driscoll. Used with permission.

291   William John Fitzgerald, *A Contemporary Celtic Prayer Book* (Chicago: ACTA, 1998), p. 19. Used with permission.

292   Anonymous, Newfoundland, Canada. Contributed by Lorna Huestis.

293   Jaci C. Maraschin, *New Gestures, New Gazes: Guide for Reading and Celebrating the Gospel of Luke*, edited by Nancy Pereira and Ernesto Cardoso, © 1993 Institute for Religious Studies, Rio de Janeiro, Brazil. Used with permission.

294   Gail Ramshaw. Used with permission.

295   NRSV.

296   Based on William S. Kervin and Lillian Perigoe. Used with permission.

302   *Voices United*, p. 837.

303   William S. Kervin; with the lines 'Life-Giver, Pain-Bearer, Love-Maker', from James Cotter, *Prayer at Night*, Cairns Publications, 1988. Used with permission.

305   William John Fitzgerald, *A Contemporary Celtic Prayer Book* (Chicago: ACTA, 1998), pp. 62–3. Used with permission.

306   William S. Kervin.

307   'Easter Evening' (verse 3), from *Enemy of Apathy* (Glasgow: Wild Goose Publications, 1988), words by John L. Bell and Graham Maule, copyright © 1988 Wild Goose Resource Group, Iona Community, Glasgow G3 2DH, Scotland. Used with permission.

309   NRSV.

310   William S. Kervin.

312   'The Song of the Supper' (chorus) from *Enemy of Apathy*
      (Glasgow: Wild Goose Publications, 1988), words by John L.
      Bell and Graham Maule, copyright © 1988 Wild Goose
      Resource Group, Iona Community, Glasgow G3 2DH,
      Scotland. Used with permission.

313   Steve Myrvang. Reprinted with permission. Excerpted from
      *Graces: Prayers and Poems for Everyday Meals and Special
      Occasions* by June Cotner (HarperSanFrancisco © 1994).

316   *Voices United*, p. 861.

317   'Heaven is Here, and earth' (Prayer of Adoration) from *A Wee
      Worship Book (Fourth Incarnation)* (Glasgow: Wild Goose
      Publications, 1999), words by John L. Bell, copyright © 1999
      Wild Goose Resource Group, Iona Community, Glasgow G3
      2DH, Scotland. Excerpted and altered by permission.

318   Judge's Grace, Honourable Society of the Middle Temple,
      England. Printed with permission of the Under Treasurer,
      Brigadier Wright.

319   'God's Table' (verse 1) from *Heaven Shall Not Wait* (Glasgow:
      Wild Goose Publications, 1987), words by John L. Bell and
      Graham Maule, copyright © 1987 Wild Goose Resource
      Group, Iona Community, Glasgow G3 2DH, Scotland. Text
      altered by permission.

321   Peter Wyatt, alt. Used with permission.

323   *Voices United*, p. 866.

324   William S. Kervin.

326   'Jesus Christ, Our Living Lord' (verse 3) from *Many and Great*
      (Glasgow: Wild Goose Publications, 1987), original text ©
      Erzebet Turmezei. Translation by John L. Bell, copyright ©
      1990 Wild Goose Resource Group, Iona Community, Glasgow
      G3 2DH, Scotland. Used with permission.

328   William John Fitzgerald, *A Contemporary Celtic Prayer Book*
      (Chicago: ACTA, 1998), pp. 85–6. Used with permission.

329   Verses 3 and 4 of 'I Come with Joy' by Brian Wren.
      Reproduced by permission of Stainer & Bell Ltd. and Hope
      Publishing Co. (United States and Canada).

330   NRSV.

331   William S. Kervin, based on *The Pattern of Our Days* edited by
      Kathy Galloway. *The Pattern of Our Days* © 1996 The Iona
      Community, published by Wild Goose Publications, Glasgow
      G2 3DH, Scotland.

332   'We Praise You for the Sun', by Alice Muriel Pullen, © 1983
      Doris M. Gill. Used with permission.

333 Based on words from Alexander Carmichael, *Carmina Gadelica: Hymns and Incantations Collected in the Highlands and Islands of Scotland in the Last Century* (Edinburgh: Floris Books, 1992, 1994).

337 NRSV.

338 William S. Kervin.

339 Words by Percy Dearmer (1867–1936) from *Enlarged Songs of Praise* 1931 by permission of Oxford University Press.

341 From Mount St Mary's Abbey, Wrentham, Mass. (based on Ecclesiastes 9.7). Used with permission.

343 Brother Thomas, alt. Nada Hermitage, Spiritual Life Institute, Crestone, Colorado. Used with permission.

344 *Voices United*, p. 868.

345 William S. Kervin, based on 'All Shall Be Well' by Kate McIlhagga from *The Pattern of Our Days*, edited by Kathy Galloway. *The Pattern of Our Days* © 1996 The Iona Community published by Wild Goose Publications, Glasgow G2 3DH, Scotland. Used with permission.

347 From Mount St Mary's Abbey, Wrentham, Mass. Used with permission.

348 The Eckhardt Family. From *One Hundred Graces* by Marcia Kelly and Jack Kelly, copyright © 1992 by Marcia Kelly and Jack Kelly. Foreword copyright © 1992 by Toinette Lippe. Used by permission of Bell Tower, a division of Random House, Inc.

349 From the Christian Renewal Center, Silverton, Oregon. Used with permission.

351 *Voices United*, p. 869.

352 William S. Kervin, based on Jan L. Richardson, *Sacred Journeys: A Woman's Book of Daily Prayer* (Nashville: Upper Room Books, 1995), p. 245.

355 William S. Kervin, based on Jan. L. Richardson, *Sacred Journeys: A Woman's Book of Daily Prayer* (Nashville: Upper Room Books, 1995), p. 244.

356 Based on words from Alexander Carmichael, *Carmina Gadelica: Hymns and Incantations Collected in the Highlands and Islands of Scotland in the Last Century* (Edinburgh: Floris Books, 1992, 1994).

357 Society of St Paul, Diocese of San Diego. Used with permission.

358 *Voices United*, p. 871.

359 William S. Kervin, inspired by Jan L. Richardson, *Sacred Journeys: A Woman's Book of Daily Prayer* (Nashville: Upper Room Books, 1995), p. 260.

361 Stephen Doyle, OFM. From *The Pilgrim's New Guide to the Holy Land* (Wilmington, Delaware: Michael Glazier Books, 1985). Used with permission of The Liturgical Press.

364 John B. Giuliani, Benedictine Grange, West Redding, Connecticut. Used with permission.

365 NRSV.

Index

Note: The numbers shown are the prayer numbers. Bible references are printed in **bold**.

141

144